To the 3rd Power

R

Reflection, Regeneration and Revitalization in the *New Millennium*

AND INTRODUCING "THE ALPHABET PRAYER"

BY DARRYL S. TUKUFU, PH.D.

To Christi
Positive thoughts
Positive action
Darl

Publisher's Note

This publication contains anecdotes and information found in speeches and/or pieces of public information taken from various audio cassettes, newspapers and books. It is marketed with the understanding that the author provided accurate and authoritative information with regard to the subject matter covered.

Books are available to organizations, corporations and professional associations at quantity discounts. For information, contact The Tukufu Group (216) 731-8451; Fax (216) 731-8453; or e-mail
dtukufu@tukufugroup.com

Cover design: Royal Fireworks Printing, Unionville, NY
Text Preparation: Royal Fireworks Printing, Unionville, NY

Publisher's Cataloging-in-Publication
(Provided by Quality Books, Inc.)
Tukufu, Darryl S.
R to the 3rd Power : reflection, regeneration
and revitalization in the new millennium / by
Darryl S. Tukufu. - 1st ed.
p. cm.
Includes bibliographical references

1.Self-actualization (Psychology)
2. Motivation (Psychology) 3. Self-help
Techniques. I. Title.

BF637.S4T85 2000158'.1
QB199-1356

The Tukufu Group   P.O. Box 43534

Richmond Heights, OH 44143

http://www.tukufugroup.com

FIRST EDITION

In Memory of

my maternal and paternal grandparents:

Peter "Pa" and Lillie "Gramma" Starks,

and
Beulah "Gramma Barm" Barham

CONTENTS

THANK YOU

Although I have been around, according to a few of my great aunts, only "a short bit of time," I have had the privilege of meeting many inspirational people. They are too numerous to list in this book, but they have inspired me, taught me, and, in numerous ways, enriched my life. However, I must give what young folks call "shout outs," or recognition, to a few of them.

First and foremost, before recognizing and thanking individuals, I must thank almighty God. Whatever I have and whatever I contribute to society and the world is because of Him. Without Him I would be nothing.

Second, I must thank my wife, Myra, who has walked next to me, sharing a partnership; walked in front of me, pulling me along; and walked behind me, pushing me forward. She has encouraged me, offered constructive criticism, and has given me the quiet time I needed to complete this book. I love you baby!

Third, I must thank my sons, Ricky and Khari Ture. Although Ricky is some distance away, residing on the West Coast, the years we spent together are memorable. He helped me understand that I must continue to develop patience and understanding, in order to relate to the younger generation. At home, Khari Ture, in his own particular way, has taught me the value of staying healthy and keeping my wits about me, because I've had to respond to the numerous questions an adolescent might ask.

Fourth, I thank my mother, Bernice Starks, for her efforts, "by any means necessary," to make sure that I knew the difference between right and wrong; my father and stepmother, Estus and Joyce Barham, for their encouragement and support in helping me overcome any obstacles; and my sister, Cheryl Golden, and step-sister, Deborah Davis, for their inspiration, support, and prayers.

Fifth, I thank my editor, Meta McMillian, for her ability to make sense out of "no sense," help pinpoint my objectives, and help me to be more concise with my ideas. There were numerous times when, after reviewing her comments or sentence changes, I would blurt out, "That's what I meant to say!"

Sixth, I thank all of my relatives and in-laws around the country. They include members of the Starks, Barham, Dean, Freeman, McDuffie, Hazely, Bates, Wells, Welch, Clark, Black, Bagley, Fitts, Walker, Webb, Duncan, Hughes, Wilkins, Ward, Bufkin, Shivers, and Jackson families.

Seventh, I thank you, the reader, for being interested enough to read this book.

INTRODUCTION

Much has been written and spoken over the years regarding the importance of having a positive mental attitude. The books and/or articles I have read on the subject, as well as the numerous self-help and motivational speakers I have heard, emphasize its significance. Being a positive thinker is both essential and effective in preparing us to live up to life's challenges, whether those challenges involve our job, family, or personal development. However, there is more to it than just being a positive thinker. Action is required.

This book is designed to help you become a better person all around, to do more than you expected to do, and obtain more than the basics you need to simply exist. I start with the premise that we all are doing something positive and have something to offer the world. However, we can do better. The old saying, "practice makes perfect," has been replaced over the years with the more applicable adage, "practice makes improvement." The reality is that we can continue to strive for it, but we can never reach perfection. We can, however, always be better than we are now. We can do more than we originally intended. Oftentimes, we just lack the direction and drive at various times in our lives to help us excel.

As you read through this book, I am sure you will discover things about yourself that you want to change. I will provide you with the tools to do so. We all need food, clothing, and shelter. However, what you will find in this book are keys to obtaining other essentials for a quality life that you may have overlooked. These other essentials include faith, surrounding yourself with positive and encouraging friends, and establishing goals and a plan of action. Having these would definitely put you on a different plane.

I decided to write this book to not only help others, but to challenge and help me become a better person as well. We can all grow and develop. A more positive attitude is available to all. I find it disheartening to run into individuals who respond to everyday questions in such a bleak manner. They get asked: "How are you?" Or, "What's happening?" They respond with: "Just trying to make it." Or, "Nothing." Those responses are so negative. There are a number of things we can say instead, like: "Great," "Great things," or "Better than some, better than most." I implore you to make the effort to return every greeting with a positive, more optimistic response. Your outlook reflects what you say. Most of us self-help advocates often refer to the maxim, "87% of our thoughts are negative," during our presentations. Therefore, I say push the envelope by striving for positive thoughts, because they will inevitably transfer into more positive statements.

Also, be prepared for encounters with negative, or perhaps toxic, people. When I mentioned the plans for this book, a few in my circle of acquaintances insinuated that they didn't like the focus. Some even suggested topics different from what I proposed. A few felt that because of my former activist background, I should focus on books and/or articles using a sociological analysis of human behavior exhibited during periods of tension, competition, and change. Although this is not a bad idea in itself, occasionally I feel far too many of us believe that everything must be analyzed within those contexts. Such views tend to leave little room to consider how individuals feel about themselves as individuals. Ultimately, I told those acquaintances that I would consider their suggestions for upcoming books.

Others who were told about my plans, often asked whether I would ever write a book about cultural diversity. This question was asked because some of my colleagues felt my first book, "*A Guide Toward the Successful Development of African-American Males,*" was too narrow in its focus. However, I contend then and now that the model I developed also works with African-American women; and, that diversity does not mean de-emphasizing who we are racially or ethnically. Nonetheless, their question did raise an interesting thought. Many books and presentations about developing a positive mental attitude tend to negate differences in race and gender, to promote the idea that we all suffer from the same sort of negative influences in our lives. Proponents of that argument say that because we are all members of one race, the human race, then our interactions and responses to various stimuli in society basically will be the same. In an ideal world, this may be true. However, acknowledging diversity allows us to put some focus on both our differences and similarities, not presenting one group and its practices as being superior over any other. I feel that recognizing racial, gender, and cultural differences, and putting them in a positive and informative light, will greatly assist us in moving out of the box(es) that enclose us. Learning about others helps ease fears and suspicions we have about them, and opens us up to embrace a wider range of individuals who could have a positive impact on our lives.

While diversity is not the focus of the book, aspects of it are included. You will find that I add diversity themes in a few sections. I make the case for how embracing diversity can be a challenge and a positive move toward developing a positive mental attitude. My argument is made without getting into drawn out discussions about "melting pots" or "pulling yourself up by the bootstraps." I believe

3

these discussions wrongly insinuate that we are all the same, rather than being as different as a bowl of stew, or tossed salad, which we really are in this society. Additionally, our problems aren't a matter of "laziness or lack of a work ethic." So let's face it. We just need to understand that being different does not mean being bad or wrong.

Although my writings are typically academic, in the appropriate venue, in this book I write as I speak, in everyday language. Most of the time I will write using "we" and "you," as a pronoun in the second person plural, to establish intimacy with the reader. The masculine and feminine pronouns, "he," "him," and "his," and "she," "her," and "hers," are used generically to refer to members of both sexes. As a human resource consultant specializing in personal growth and development, organizational development, and diversity management, I am cognizant of the importance and use of language for "inclusion" rather than "exclusion." Thus, I prefer to include my audience as much as I can when conducting these sessions. I also find it is easier to communicate using this method for the purposes of this book.

I selected the title, *"R to the Third Power: Reflection, Regeneration and Revitalization in the New Millennium,"* because all of the developmental and success oriented main topics I chose begin with the letter "R." Each topic has important meanings for personal growth.

The section on Reflection emphasizes the need to evaluate where we are developmentally at this point in our lives. It assists us in answering such questions as: "Am I the kind of person I want to be?" Have I progressed over the years?" and "Am I stuck in a rut?" I utilize two analytical tools I developed to assist us with our self-reflection: a Feelings Inventory and an analysis we will use in the last section of the book.

4

Following our self-analysis, we will segue to a section on establishing a foundation, a beginning or continuing effort, that leads to that positive mental attitude we seek. I call this section Regeneration, since it focuses on a spiritual and/or religious foundation that is essential in the development process. There are those who believe that *all* we need is this foundation. In an ideal world, they are correct. However, we find that in the real world followers of different faiths need a little more assistance to achieve their goal, to be better persons. Troubled and negative individuals exist in different religious and spiritual settings, as in other places. Other supplementary elements that are a part of the self-improvement process are included in various other segments in the book. However, it's in Regeneration that I first introduce one of the seven key points, in developing a positive attitude, that are spotlighted in *"R to the Third Power."* That point is to *Have Faith.*

The last section is Revitalization. This section presents the six other points necessary to obtain a positive mental attitude, and thus success on all levels. These points are *Encourage Yourself, Surround Yourself with Quality People, Don't Trip, Avoid the Comfort Zone_Work, Set Your Goals and Objectives,* and *Have a Plan of Action.*

I believe that if you follow the instructions contained throughout the book, you will rise to new heights. You will feel better than you ever thought you could. You will enter a room with a new strut. You will be more than another face in any place. So, if you're ready, let's begin the process!

REFLECTION

It is my belief that prior to engaging in a process leading to personal growth and success, an individual should undergo some self-analysis, and get feedback from persons who are well known to her. I call this self-analytical aspect reflection, because it allows individuals to be introspective, open-minded, and think positively about the feedback they receive. How can we determine which direction we should take if we do not know where we are right now? Many of us probably have been lost at some point in our lives. I recall times when I traveled to other cities and I either misread the directions, didn't follow the directions as I should have, or was given the wrong directions. If I had stopped at a gas station or asked a passerby for help, someone would begin by first saying where I was at that moment. Even if I had called someone already at my final destination, that person would first find out where I was. Thus, we have to first know where we are before we can move ahead.

To help us find where we are, I have developed two processes, a Feelings Inventory and an analysis to assist us in setting our goals and objectives, and in preparing a plan of action.

I define feelings as subjective reactions or responses to situations. The subjective aspect makes it more personal. That is, our feelings are our feelings. They are personal. We have ownership of them, and will more than likely act the same way in similar circumstances unless we decide to change how we respond or react. However, our feelings can change. If you believe this is false then try to count the number of times you have said, "I'll never do that."

Like many of us you probably find yourself doing whatever you said you would not do.

Below, you will find a Feelings Inventory that I developed for this section. It is designed to set the tone for self-reflection. It will assist you in determining where you are at this point in your life, and provide you with some feedback toward a more "preferable" state. Please complete this inventory, but I would also suggest that if you prefer a more in-depth assessment, with statistical validity and reliability, that you should investigate those that are available in the market.

Once you complete the inventory, go to the next section where I introduce another analytical tool that I developed. This analysis, combined with your responses to the feelings inventory, will assist you in the last stages of Revitalization, that is in developing your goals and objectives, and formulating a plan of action.

Now, proceed to the Feelings Inventory. Please, do not read further or try to peek at the "preferable" responses. Your answers are correct because they are "your" responses, so they can't be wrong. One more thing, please use a pencil because in the future your responses may change. Also, make copies of the forms and questionnaires to use if the copy of the book you're reading is borrowed.

FEELINGS INVENTORY

The following list is composed of a series of statements about feelings. If a statement describes how you usually feel, put an x in the column "like me." If a statement does not describe how you usually feel, put an x in the column "unlike me."

LIKE ME   **UNLIKE ME**

LIKE ME	UNLIKE ME	
____	____	1. MOST OF MY PEERS LIKE ME.
____	____	2. I'M EASILY RILED BY PROBLEMS I FACE.
____	____	3. MANY PEOPLE FEEL THAT I AM A FUN PERSON TO BE AROUND.
____	____	4. THERE ARE MANY THINGS I WOULD CHANGE ABOUT MYSELF.
____	____	5. MOST OF THE TIME, I AM QUIET AND RESERVED IN A GROUP.
____	____	6. I WORRY A LOT ABOUT WHAT PEOPLE SAY ABOUT ME.
____	____	7. MOST OF THE TIME I GIVE IN, IN ORDER TO AVOID CONFLICT.
____	____	8. I'M HARD ON MYSELF IF I DON'T DO A GOOD JOB.
____	____	9. I'M PRETTY VOCAL WHEN IT COMES TO EXPRESSING MY OPINION.
____	____	10. MY FRIENDS AND/OR FAMILY ARE TOO DEMANDING OF MY TIME.
____	____	11. THERE ARE MANY TIMES I JUST WANT TO SAY "FORGET IT" AND THEN MOVE ON.

8

_____ _____ 12. THE TRUTH IS, I WISH I WERE SOMEONE ELSE.

_____ _____ 13. MY FAMILY AND/OR THOSE I CONSIDER CLOSE TO ME SHOW CONCERN FOR MY FEELINGS.

_____ _____ 14. IT'S HARD TO JUST BE THE WAY I WANT TO BE.

_____ _____ 15. MOST PEOPLE I COME IN CONTACT WITH KNOW WHERE I'M COMING FROM.

_____ _____ 16. I'M ALWAYS NOTICED WHEN I'M IN A GROUP.

_____ _____ 17. I'M KNOWN AS A PERSON WHO ALWAYS FOLLOWS THROUGH.

_____ _____ 18. I GET UPSET PRETTY EASILY.

_____ _____ 19. MOST OF THE TIME I HAVE POSITIVE THOUGHTS.

_____ _____ 20. MANY PEOPLE I INTERACT WITH LOOK TO ME TO COME UP WITH IDEAS OR THINGS TO DO.

_____ _____ 21. THERE ARE MANY OCASSIONS WHEN I WISH THAT I WAS OF A DIFFERENT RACE AND/OR ETHNICITY.

_____ _____ 22. THERE ARE MANY OCASSIONS WHERE I WISH THAT I WAS OF A DIFFERENT GENDER/SEX.

_____ _____ 23. I AM CONTENT WITH AND HAVE NO PROBLEM IF OTHERS KNOW OF MY SEXUAL ORIENTATION.

_____ _____ 24. I NEVER WANT TO FEEL OLD.

IF APPLICABLE:

_____ _____ 25. THERE ARE MANY TIMES I BELIEVE THAT MY DISABILITY OR BEING "PHYSICALLY CHALLENGED" PREVENTS ME FROM HAVING POSITIVE RELATIONSHIPS WITH OTHERS.

As I mentioned prior to your completion of the inventory, "your" answer is correct for you, thus, there is no scoring attached to this exercise. I do, however, suggest some "preferred" responses, which I believe are preferable in order for us to develop positive feelings about ourselves. I want you to reflect on your answers and take particular note of the preferable responses and brief explanations that follow. If you find something about yourself that you want to change, just understand that it will not happen overnight. We can and will develop a step-by-step process to get you where you want to be.

"PREFERABLE" ANSWER KEY:

1. LIKE ME. Although peers can be viewed as anyone who has "equal standing" with us, most of the time use of this term refers to companions, friends, or acquaintances. We tend to feel better about ourselves if these individuals appear to like us. Although many of us may know of someone who says, "I don't care what anyone thinks of me," the truth is that this statement more likely is a telltale to the contrary. They probably do care about what their peers think of them, but use the "I don't care" statement as a defense mechanism. Believing that your peers like and support you will help you in obtaining a more positive outlook on life.

2. UNLIKE ME. A "like me" response obviously shows that you are easily riled by your problems, which is further evidence that you exercise little control over your feelings. Thus, an "unlike me" response would be preferable, because it indicates that you have or exercise some control over your situation(s).

3. LIKE ME. At first glance, one would think I am making a distinction between introverts and extroverts. That is not the case. Both introverts and extroverts can be fun to be with, or can be no fun at all. However, many of us have a good sense of how others feel about us. Some will tell us verbally, while others will let us know with their body language.

4. UNLIKE ME. The key word here is "many." Most of us are aware of something about ourselves that we would like to change. However, when it is quite a few things, this suggests that we do not have positive feelings about our capabilities.

10

5. UNLIKE ME. Recall that this is a feeling point. Furthermore, the key word here is "most." A sense of inadequacy can be felt to the extent that you will be uncomfortable even around individuals with whom you are well acquainted.

6. UNLIKE ME. Worry is uneasiness and uncertainty, which can have a crippling effect on individuals. Many years ago, I found that when I worried about what people were saying about me, it caused me mental stress and physical tension. This led to loss of sleep and a reluctance to be around people. I also found myself constantly on the defensive when interacting with others.

7. UNLIKE ME. "Giving in" sometimes is not bad when we are attempting to arrive at some compromise. But, giving in most of the time, to avoid disputes, may make us feel good temporarily, but that feeling may not last. I've found that many individuals who give in really wish they could have stood up for themselves. They are the ones who say, "I should have" or "I could have" after the fact.

8. UNLIKE ME. There is nothing wrong with critiquing yourself and being critiqued by others. A problem arises when we do this constantly. One thing that will help is to get legitimate feedback_either from reports, a successful program or venture, etc.

9. LIKE ME. This, in one sense, is the flip side of number five above. Even if your opinion is simply that, an opinion, the fact you have expressed it makes you feel good about yourself.

10. UNLIKE ME. A "like me" response indicates that we allow individuals to be demanding of our time. It puts them in control, and we allow it. We may want to say how we really feel, but may not, for fear of hurting feelings. Meanwhile, we feel powerless and may wind up not trying to change that situation at all.

11. UNLIKE ME. Wanting to move on is not bad in itself. However, when it becomes a dominant feeling, then it begins to erode our sense of being in control. Avoiding challenges is a failure to bring closure to the different situations we face.

12. UNLIKE ME. Of all the situations in this inventory, this one may be the easiest to understand. Wishing that you were someone else definitely indicates that you have negative feelings about yourself. You may feel that challenges are too overwhelming because of who you are now, that

you just don't like who you see in the mirror, as well as many more situations you encounter that contribute to this negative self-image.

13. LIKE ME. Feeling that our family and friends are concerned about our feelings makes us feel good, wanted, and important. It does a lot to encourage us to open up and talk about things that trouble us, and gives us a boost in confidence.

14. UNLIKE ME. There are certain "ways" that many of us would like to freely exhibit. Believing that it's impossible to show our true selves, saps our energy, and leaves us open to further challenges that may be difficult to overcome. Feeling that it's easy to "be me," and still be accepted by others, provides us with a form of power and therefore an additional source of strength.

15. LIKE ME. A feeling that we are understood, raises our self-esteem and self-image. It assists us in overcoming barriers to our development.

16. LIKE ME. When I was younger, my mother and teachers would always say "walk straight and tall and you will stand out in the crowd." They were partially correct. When we walk in this manner, we have a good chance of standing out. However, we really stand out because of an air of confidence we exude, in what we say, and in our overall demeanor. Our sense of confidence draws attention to us.

17. LIKE ME. Following through on what we said we would do, or accomplish, makes us and those around us feel good. And because others think highly of us, we automatically begin to think well of ourselves. If people constantly remind us in word or deed that we are a person who can't be counted on, this will reflect negatively on how we see ourselves.

18. UNLIKE ME. I have told many people that this book is therapy for me, just as much as it is for people I am trying to help. My own response to this is contrary to what I know to be the preferable approach. Responding that this is "like me" means that it is something I have to work on continually. It represents a flaw, a retreat of sorts from positive feelings. When this happens, it detracts us from further development and movement toward success.

19. LIKE ME. See number 18, above.

20. LIKE ME. This response shows that you have leadership qualities, and that others value your opinions.

21. UNLIKE ME. To respond "like me" is to indicate that you have problems or misgivings about your race, which is often the case among people of color, because of tremendous acculturation and assimilation pressures in this society. There is a need to have positive race-esteem in conjunction with positive self-esteem.

22. UNLIKE ME. To respond "like me" is to indicate a problem with gender identity, or there is gender confusion. This may impact you in negative ways, unless you respond "like me" in number 23.

23. LIKE ME. This response shows a healthy recognition of self, in spite of individual and societal problems, around this issue. Such openness may be difficult to handle if your sexual/affectional orientation is not considered "straight." If you are considered "different," and you respond "unlike me," then your issues have been identified by that response. Ideally, you must come to terms with your orientation, or it will cause you great stress.

24. UNLIKE ME. Responding in this fashion infers that you can grow older, and not be bothered by it.

25. UNLIKE ME. There are difficulties faced by the physically challenged that are sometimes unimaginable. But if you are in this situation, it can adversely affect your ability to thrive if you always ask yourself, "Is this person with me because she feels sorry for me or does she want to truly be my friend?"

As I mentioned above, this is the first step in Reflection. I want you to now proceed to the next analysis.

A method, or process, used by both public and private sector organizations in developing their strategic plans is called the SWOT analysis. SWOT stands for strengths, weaknesses, opportunities and threats. This process allows an organization to use such categories to describe and determine its current operational status, to help managers de-

13

termine where that organization wants to go in the future.

After utilizing this process quite frequently in my work with organizations, I have determined that the process can also be applied to individuals. Thus, I have developed a variant of SWOT, which I call a SCOB analysis. SCOB stands for strengths, challenges, opportunities and barriers, as categories to analyze individuals. I chose "challenges" over "weaknesses," because I prefer the use of positive sounding analytical tools, particularly in relation to individuals. In my opinion, words and terminology are very important because they have connotative and denotative meanings. Using the term "weaknesses," I believe, implies that something debilitating, with a large degree of powerlessness, may be inherent in an individual. Therefore, individuals may not be able to perform successfully because they may believe that it is something innately wrong with them. Calling something a weakness seems to indicate it will always be a point of failure in a person's life. Calling it a challenge leaves room for hope. Similarly, I think that "threats" may be a little too strong a descriptive tool in referring to individuals and their actions, and thus chose the word "barriers."

In strategic planning with organizations, I use the SWOT analysis, but add another point of inquiry. Thus, a form of this analysis is called SWOT+1. So the adapted process I use for individuals in this particular exercise is called SCOB+1. The +1 indicates that another question can be proposed in the process. Additionally, although individuals complete the analysis on themselves, they are also encouraged to have individuals, who know them quite well, complete the analysis about the individual in question. I'm not sure where I heard it, but there is a saying that goes, "If one person calls you a jackass, you can just about ignore it. However, if ten people call you one you had better look for a saddle to wear." For our purposes, the five will replace the ten, and they should be just as consistent in the points they make concerning you.

The SCOB+1 analysis follows. Before you read further, I strongly urge you to complete the analysis right now. On a separate piece of paper, give the questions to five people of your choosing, first changing the "my" in each question and adding your name. Ask the individuals you select to complete their analysis of you within seven days. It does not matter if their responses reflect personal or professional opinions about you. All of the information you receive will be utilized. You can decide to read further in this book, after your own analysis, or wait until you receive your outside analyses. At any rate, you will need to have both your and the other responses to be able to complete the segment presented later on *Setting Your Goals and Objectives,* and *Have a Plan of Action*, respectively.

Now, let's begin with the questions:

1. What are my **strengths**?

_____

_____

_____

_____

_____

2. What are my **challenges**?

_____

_____

_____

_____

3. If I maximize my strengths and minimize those things that challenge me, or are difficult, what **opportunities** do I see developing for me in the next few years?

_____

_____

_____

_____

_____

_____

4. What **barriers** do I see that will prevent me from taking advantage of these opportunities?

_____

_____

_____

_____

_____

5. **+1** How should I prepare myself for the future?

_____

_____

_____

_____

REGENERATION

The second R in *R to the Third Power* is Regeneration. The word "regenerate" has a number of meanings. A couple of these meanings are renewal and reviving. For our purposes, I refer to the usage of this word to represent spiritual and/or religious rebirth or conversion, and reaching or restoring us to a higher state. In that light, spiritual regeneration as a process is important in developing a positive mental attitude and moving toward success in whatever goals we set.

In this section, I will mainly comment on two of the most significant aspects of regeneration referred to above, namely spirituality and religion. Additionally, I will introduce the first of seven critical points leading to positive mental attitude, the first being *Have Faith*. The final six points will be included in the last R segment, Revitalization.

Spirituality and Religion

Although my mother informed me that I was christened as a child, I did not become a follower of Christ and later become baptized until age 31. When I was young and living in Cleveland, Ohio, I recall visiting a number of churches. But at that time, I was more interested in looking at the females in attendance. Additionally, just as many other people did, I celebrated holidays mainly because they were another day off work. My religious awakening of sorts came later, when I was a little older, and had moved to California. In 1967, after graduating from high school in Los Angeles, I joined the Los Angeles-based Us Organization, a Black cultural nationalist group. I professed a belief in Kawaida, a faith established by Dr. Maulana Karenga, who is the founder of Us, the Nguzo Saba (Seven Principles of the Black Value System), and the African-American celebration of Kwanzaa. This faith was based on African spirituality. Later, for an eight to ten-year stretch, somewhere between the early 70's and 1980, I fancied myself an agnostic.

I consider myself spiritual and religious today, because of my Christian beliefs. Although both concepts have an ecclesiastic aspect, notably a degree of formality, I interpret spirituality as broader in scope than religion. Spirituality is a state of mind connecting us to God, the creator. It is an important aspect of virtually all religions or faiths. Additionally, because spiritual principles and practices are inextricably bound to the life and living process, being spiritual strengthens our character so that we act differently from those who do not profess a spiritual base. Spiritual persons acknowledge that a positive, spiritual force, rather than our own possibly negative tendencies, leads us in the proper direction. For example, a spiritual force opens the way for hate to evolve to love, violence to peace, and doubt to trust.

Furthermore, having a spiritual base greatly assists in bonding people of various faiths for a joint effort or cause. Thus, from a diversity viewpoint, we may see followers of Judaism, Christianity, Islam, Buddhism, Ba'hai, Yoruba, or other indigenous African or Eastern religions, etc., working together in peace and harmony. They are united by a belief in a spiritual force that works for the good in all of wo(man)kind.

While spirituality is a state of mind, religion is the form of service and worship of God in an institutionalized system with concomitant beliefs, attitudes, and practices. And although religions have a spiritual base, aspects of religion are at once general and specific in how that spirituality is expressed. For example Christians are generally followers of Christ, but have specific denominations that have different attitudes and practices. The same applies to followers of Judaism, Islam and other faiths.

Regeneration is important because it taps into that source of inner strength, that basis, we need for a successful life. If spirituality and religion are lacking in our lives, we will be hindered from obtaining the good life that's not necessarily determined by wealth and materialism, but by a balance of spirit and possessions. Having balance allows us to attend to all areas in our lives, without giving undue attention to any one area.

Next, we will look at the first of the seven critical points, that I mentioned earlier, that we need to develop a positive mental attitude. I title the first point *Have Faith*, which is incorporated here in R2, Regeneration.

1. HAVE FAITH

I am quite sure that many of you who have heard Ministers, Imams, Rabbis, Priests or other spiritual leaders talk about *belief* and *faith*. I thought, like many others, that these words were synonymous. However, they are best interpreted as two sides of the same coin, with their own particular meanings.

I consider belief as the thinking side, a state of mind or concurrence with an established pattern of thought. Belief, or to believe, is to internalize convictions that one interprets as facts. Therefore, when one believes something one has no doubts about it. It is true to that person, and usually there is little anyone can say or do to dissuade him. Within a spiritual context, for example, one may talk about believing the written word of God. The problem is that far too many simply believe, but move no further than that. That is why I say we must put the emphasis on faith!

Faith is the "doing" side of the coin, the action. In other words, acting on what you believe. Not long ago, I spoke during a Men's Day program in a church in Cleveland. I asked members of the congregation to raise their hands if they believed in God. Then I asked them to raise their hands if they had faith. Virtually the same hands were raised both times. I then recited my version of faith, using a story that's similar to one written by Dr. Frederick Price in his book *"How Faith Works."* My version is a little different, and I change it to fit my audience. In this case I asked the congregation to imagine_

Service is over and you have been worshipping God all morning. Most of the congregation moves to the Fellowship Hall where there is a pretty elaborate reception. All of a sudden a man from the surrounding neighborhood walks in and falls out. Sister Jackson, who is a medical doctor, examines him and says that this man must eat immediately or he will die. Some of the choir members in attendance began singing "Rise Up and Walk." The man comes to, the doctor explains her diagnosis to the man, and the deacons there ask him over and over: "Do you believe if you eat you will live?"

At the same time, the pastor and a visiting evangelist start praising God for the man's visit. They ask the man, "Do you believe in God?" The man responds, "No, I don't." However, members of the congregation continue following the deacons' lead and asks the man, "Do you believe that if you eat you will live?" The man says, "I believe that if I eat I will live." Then, over and over he says, "I believe it, I believe it, I believe it."

20

All of a sudden the man collapses, and Sister Jackson says, "We have lost him."

So, what happened? Everyone believed. The choir, Pastor and the Evangelist started feeding the man spiritual food, although he wasn't receptive. The Deacons and others present worked on getting him to believe that if he ate physical food he would live. The man, obviously wanting to save himself, at least physically, stated he believed that if he ate he would live. But what happened?

A couple of points can be made. First, to respond to the question I posed, nothing happened. There was no action! The food was present but the man did not eat, although he believed it would save him. Moreover, the church members did not even try to feed him. They believed, just as he did, that if he ate he would be all right. Everyone was stuck on believing. Neither he nor the church members had faith. Not one of them "acted" on what they believed.

Second, the man passed away without a spiritual base. He stated that he did not believe in God. In this scenario, a dilemma may have been created within him, because he was being asked questions on two different issues, on whether he believed in God and whether eating the food would save him. He responded affirmatively to what he may have believed was the most pressing need at that time, simply to eat. Sometimes it is this need that must be satisfied before we can move a step or two further. I learned many years ago that it may be better to first win the person, rather than the point. Once we win the person, we can usually come back later and win the point. However, in this story the man was lost both ways.

21

I will tell you another story, a personal one, that relates to faith in the natural realm. When I was younger I took a number of swimming lessons. Some were at city swimming pools and others at day camp or overnight camps. Over a period of ten years, I learned to hold my breath and do both the dead man's and jellyfish float. However, everything I did was in shallow water.

A number of swimming instructors tried to explain to me how easy it was to swim in deep water. Also, I watched both young people and senior citizens dive into the water and move all around like it was nothing at all. Throughout these years, I did believe. I believed that if I moved my hands, arms, legs, and feet the way other swimmers did I would be able to swim in deep water. But, I did not venture out into the deep end of the pool, unless I stayed along the side. I would kick my legs like I was really doing something. However, I held onto the side of the pool, and if anyone asked me how I was doing with my swimming lessons, I would say, "I'm swimming in deep water." I didn't dare tell them that I was scared of the deep end, and that I held onto the side for dear life. Neither would I tell them that if someone threatened to push or pull me away from the sides, and into the deep water of the swimming pool, I would immediately vacate the pool.

As it turned out, the day finally came when I had to act and thereby show my faith in what I said I believed all along. I was a student at Los Angeles City College, and had enrolled in a swimming class to fulfill a physical education requirement. To pass this course you had to swim, tread water, and dive into the deep end. You should have seen me! With little hesitation I jumped into the deep end and was surprised at how easy it was for me. I was so bold I jumped a number of times off the 20-foot-high diving board. All the while I kept thinking about all of the years

22

I wasted in the shallow water, just because I did not move to the point of taking the action required by faith.

Although I have pointed out the difference between belief and faith on a number of occasions, many people continue to feel that believing is sufficient. A few note the beauty and the power of such songs as "You've Got to Believe in Yourself," sung in the Broadway musical and movie version of "The Wiz." Then, there is R. Kelly singing, "I believe I Can Fly," that is so inspirational. There's nothing wrong with these songs or with emphasizing believing. As I said, belief and faith are two sides of the same coin. However, I feel putting too much emphasis on merely believing is half-stepping. You've got to take the full step, both the spiritual and secular. You won't get anything if you just believe. You've got to put the pedal to the metal! You've got to move and groove! You've got to get off your duff and do your stuff! And all of this means FAITH_ AC-TION!

Now, after saying all of this I must point out that having faith will not cure all of our ills, or remove all of our obstacles. In this world, we all are likely to suffer from all sorts of injustices at times. Things will happen in our lives that we have no power to change or control. Obstacles will not disappear just because we say, "I have faith." But that doesn't mean we shouldn't try to overcome them. What we still must do is rely on the strength of God, and act on the things we can change.

Think about the seed that is among the smallest of all seeds_the mustard seed, and how in ancient Palestine it grew into the largest of the garden plants. Therefore, if the adage "you of little faith" fits you at this point in your life, work to strengthen your faith. Continue to look up, because if you can see your way up like that mustard seed, you can grow to be just as tall and strong.

In the first section I discussed Reflection. You responded to what I call the SCOB +1 analysis, and you obtained feedback from at least five people close to you, on how you are perceived by them. Prior to this exercise, you identified certain personal feelings from my Feelings Inventory. Undoubtedly, toxins were identified that you need to get rid of from your mental health system. Realize that these poisons can and will retard your growth_spiritually, mentally, and emotionally. Also, these toxins will affect your physical health.

For this process of self-development to work, you must understand and reckon with these truths. Doing this makes it easier for you to become spiritually in tune with yourself. Becoming spiritually attuned is accomplished through prayer and meditation. Another helpful tool, something that I have recently become acquainted with, is called Reiki, a hands-on healing and relaxation technique that I will discuss a little later.

But first, there is prayer. Prayer is an essential way to reach the spiritual renewal that we need. Prayer is a means to talk with, give thanks to, and make formal requests to God. It is not always a matter of begging, but is a necessary aspect of worship. I must also emphasize how important it is to schedule a time to pray, or it will not happen. Furthermore, it must not become a stiff formality. An approach, which may help you as it does me, is to "plan your praying, then pray your plan." As a guide, I wrote the following prayer to assist me in asking for those qualities, attributes, etc. that I need to become a God-inspired individual.

THE ALPHABET PRAYER

I pray for continuous *A*wakening to the truth of who God is and what He stands for.

I pray for *B*alance that will assist me in focusing on all necessary aspects of life.

I pray for *C*ompassion that will enable me to understand others' distress and seek ways to alleviate it.

I pray for *D*iscernment that will reveal to me things that are hidden but divine.

I pray for patient *E*ndurance to stay the course and follow the principles of my belief.

I pray for *F*aith...the ability to act on what I believe.

I pray for *G*race, the transforming power and divine assistance that will lead me toward spiritual renewal.

I pray for *H*umility, the spirit of deference needed for the will of God to be visible in my life.

I pray for *I*llumination that will bring about divine edification.

I pray that I will do all that is necessary to prepare for *J*udgment Day.

I pray for *K*nowledge, which will lead toward good judgment.

I pray that I will be able to *L*ive the life of a true believer.

I pray that I will be forever *M*indful and provide assistance to the poor and oppressed.

I pray for continued *N*ourishment that is provided by a strong spiritual base.

I pray that I will not be *O*verbearing or quick-tempered.

I pray for *P*atience in the midst of overwhelming affliction.

I pray for God-fearing *Q*uality people to surround me at all times.

I pray for *R*econciliation_a changed relationship with God where my trespasses will not be counted against me.

I pray for continuing *S*alvation and results, which will lead to a God-centered life.

I pray for *T*ruth, a constant pursuit of a transcendent spiritual reality.

I pray for *U*nderstanding, composed of spiritual and intellectual knowledge and comprehension.

I pray for *V*irtue, so that I can be a model of strength and an example of moral excellence.

I pray for *W*isdom, which added to knowledge and understanding, will lead me to God-directed action.

I pray for eXuberance, indicating that I am joyously unrestrained and exhibit enthusiastic faith.

Finally, I pray for continuous Youthful vigor to fight the good fight, to finish the race, in order to fulfill the necessary prerequisites to reach the ultimate Zenith marked by my departing this physical life.

Meditation, in a spiritual sense, is our means of listening to God. To listen to God we must be quiet, and release fleeting thoughts, that some people call mind chatter. However, meditation has other benefits. Research indicates that meditation can reduce heart rate and blood pressure, decrease our stress levels, and improve immune functions.

Although meditation appears to be a simple activity to perform, many people find it very challenging. A few of the reasons people give for not engaging in meditation are skepticism about its benefits, boredom at the idea of sitting still for a long time, and time constraints. But one can meditate in many different ways. Some practitioners advocate being still and silent at the same time. They discourage you from having any thoughts. They purport that meditation, as a form of healing, means inactivity. They emphasize not only letting go of current thoughts, but also resisting any new ones that come to you.

Others advocate a form of vocalizing, initially by repeating the simple sentence "I am." Any positive thoughts that come to mind are welcomed. Thus, a person can utter a number of self-affirming sentences, such as "I am blessed," "I am strong and determined," "I am able to achieve in spite of circumstances," etc. Another vocaliza-

27

tion exercise involves repeating over and over such phrases as "relax, let go," while breathing deeply. Meditation exercises often are combined with breathing exercises - sometimes counting your breaths - and concentrating on some sort of image.

The use of images is popular during meditation. An image I began using a while ago, is the one of me sitting on the beach in Seaside, Oregon. Our family used to visit this beach when we lived in Portland, Oregon. It is a beautiful site to behold, and, while meditating, I would recall a special moment I experienced there. I focused on the time I would sit on the beach alone, with picturesque mountains in the background and the sun setting out over the Pacific Ocean. After my wife and I took a recent trip to Cancun, Mexico, I also started using a meditative image of the time I sat on the beach along the Caribbean Sea and watched the sea gulls and fish. You, no doubt, can recall peaceful or beautiful moments that can be used during your meditations.

One final spiritual and "healing" process I recommend you investigate is Reiki. As I mentioned earlier, Reiki is a powerful and ancient hands-on healing and relaxation technique. I attended my first Reiki "sampler" in the summer of 1999, in Cleveland, Ohio, conducted by Reiki Master Constance Haqq. According to Haqq, the Japanese developed Reiki centuries ago. Reiki means universal life force energy, and it is designed to stimulate self-healing by connecting the energy systems of the body more directly with the universal life force energy.

In the session I attended, Haqq and another Reiki master, JoAnn Horton, laid their hands on me as I lay fully clothed. They asked if there were any areas on my body that caused me pain. I responded that I had sports-related injuries that caused me pain in my shoulder and thigh. They had me concentrate on a geographical location that brought me comfort. I concentrated on Seaside, Oregon. Later they asked me what I concentrated on, and when I told them they stated water sources were good because water represents healing. During the 15-minute "sampler," I experienced a warming sensation, particularly in the areas where had I experienced pain and where they had concentrated their hands-laying exercise. I should note that even prior to the session, the pain I felt was never constant, but I could move my body in certain ways and feel it instantly. I deliberately made these pain-inducing movements after I left the session to see if there was any change. I found that the pain had subsided to some degree. But one session does not eliminate the pain entirely. According to Haqq, you would have to make appointments for follow-up sessions, just as you would with a doctor.

I was also informed by the masters that I had energy clogged in my knees. This was of great interest to me because I have had problems with my knees for as long as I can remember, but I didn't mention that to them at the outset. I was also surprised when they identified, on their own, which knee I had the most problem with. But the inner feeling I had from the sampler was also unbelievable. I was in a deeply relaxing and meditative state. Haqq explained that this state provides a foundation for deeper physical, emotional and/or spiritual healing. Additionally, these healing sessions are focused on the individual. You are not in a group session, but in an office setting where you lay on a doctor's table, once on your back and then on your stomach.

Admittedly, I went into the session somewhat skeptical about the technique, but came out of it believing that Reiki has great value. There is a real spiritual function in this type of treatment. And, it doesn't mean you have to change your religious faith or belief. Note, particularly in Christianity, there is a "laying on of hands" in many denominations. I, for one, did not feel that Reiki was only for those who believe in Eastern religions. One of my goals in writing this self-help book was to explore the tremendous diversity of personal development strategies that exist, that are available to all people. I do not think we can limit ourselves if something can work for us. Now, if it doesn't work for you that is an entirely different issue.

The strategies that I include in this book, as with my presentations, are techniques that I use to benefit my audience as well as myself. I am careful to always make that point. Therefore, when I give a suggestion as to what could assist you, I have taken the advice myself, and found it useful. Many members in my family have always said, "You're so hyper, we can't even see you relaxing or sitting still for even a short while." I have to admit that I am very active and meditation was at first difficult for me. At this writing, I am still trying to increase the number of minutes I meditate. But I also feel it has value, and I am committed to making it a daily ritual.

This is why having faith, which includes taking action, is so important. In addition to providing us with the spiritual connection that we sorely need, faith and action, along with prayer, meditation, and now Reiki can help provide us with peace of mind, a sense of meaning and tremendous health and energy.

REVITALIZATION

In the previous two sections, we began our process by first reflecting on and analyzing where we are at this point in our lives. Next, we discussed Regeneration, about ways to connect spiritually and religiously. Establishing this connection was the starting point for the seven points I have determined are necessary to develop a positive mental attitude. Now, we arrive at this last section, Revitalization. Revitalization is synonymous to rekindling, or renovating. If life were a staircase, the points emphasized in this section would be the final steps to the top. At each step, we should feel invigorated and inspired to be better than we are now.

Put another way, I liken *"R to the Third Power"* to building a home. Reflecting can be viewed as taking a careful look at your building site, determining the lay of the land, and the benefits and possible detriments to placing the home in that particular location. Regeneration is equivalent to laying down the foundation. The foundation must be as sturdy as possible or the house will fall after it's completed. Then we come to Revitalization, putting on the final touches, all of the external pieces, such as the windows, siding, etc. If the house is truly sturdy, with the grace of God, it will be able to withstand whatever elements it faces. It's through a building process such as this that you should be left feeling strong, sturdy, confident and willing to take on other pursuits.

2. ENCOURAGE YOURSELF

There is no way we can deny it. We live in a troubled world. Most of us know that many people's basic needs are not being met. Everyday we hear or read about the problems we face in society, collectively and individually. A number of these problems are related to inequality, poverty, unemployment, and underemployment. Others we encounter are based on race and racial inequality, gender roles and sex discrimination, and health and medical care. Many of us are in an uproar concerning problems of crime and law enforcement, homelessness, mental illness, and drug addiction. Work and a sense of alienation causes us concern when we are on our job. Environmental and urban problems scream at us on the way to work. And finally, we grow extremely nervous when we talk about the nuclear age and the potential technological problems in the new millennium.

This book is not a treatise on how to remedy these problems. There are movements and organizations pressing to cure these ills, and they should be supported. Fortunately, individual support is realized through views expressed in opinion polls to the effect that the majority of people want conditions to be better. But for them to be better, we as individuals also must become better. Thus, we must encourage ourselves, and there are many ways to do this.

How do you encourage yourself? Do you talk to yourself? If you do, do you talk back to yourself? Most people will not admit to talking back to themselves. I think they heard the same thing I did, "It's okay to talk to yourself, but don't talk back to yourself. You are crazy if you do." I disagree. I say talk back to yourself. In many cases you may be the only person, for awhile, that will encourage you.

If you recall my personal swimming story mentioned earlier, I had to talk back to myself. When I was telling myself "I don't want to go into the deep water," I would then follow that up by reminding myself: "Boy, you had better get in there. You wasted all of that time 'trying' to swim but didn't do anything. Besides, remember your grade counts on your getting out there."

This also brings to mind times when men would sit around and talk about how they can't understand women. I heard this when I was younger and still hear it today, when I conduct sessions with men on "redefining masculinity." One recurring source of confusion for men is why women ask questions, or speak aloud to no one in particular, for instance, about what they are going to wear to an event? Men I work with cite other questions that women would ask them, or just blurt out, such as: "I wonder how this would look?" "Am I matching?" "I wonder if someone else will be wearing this same outfit?" "Do I need to wear different color shoes?" The point is that in some cases the man had to respond. At other times, the woman would answer the question herself. They would say: "Heck, I'm going to wear this outfit no matter what!"

But men also have their moments. The questions they ask may be directed to others, but many times men may likewise direct the questions to themselves. For example, if men have strong feelings about a woman, they may wonder out loud about how she felt about their date, if she's dating someone else, what she thinks of him and if he has bad breath. I think you get the picture. Some men, with a lot of bravado, will answer themselves with, "No problem. She acted like she really liked me." Or, "No sweat, how could she resist me?" The point is we talk to ourselves, privately or otherwise, at times, so why not talk to ourselves to boost our self-image.

Encouraging you is essentially building your self-image and self-esteem. And our self-image does not operate in a vacuum. So many other aspects of our lives depend on how we view ourselves. Our self-image affects our attitudes and behaviors. Essentially, the concept of self-image relates to how we see ourselves in our various roles. For example, I see myself as a Christian, a heterosexual, a husband, a father, a brother, an entrepreneur, just to name a few. In all of these roles I am performing at optimum when my self-esteem is healthy, i.e., positive. I have found that to the degree I am confident in my role, I am also competent. Thus, when the image of myself in a particular role is very good to excellent, I perform accordingly. And vice versa. If my image is only good, fair or poor, I respond in kind.

Although I have been a follower of Christ some 19 years, I have had some difficult moments with my self-image, especially during religious activities. If I am called on to pray or give grace, for example, my prayer can be very short. The problem is that I don't feel confident quoting scripture. I feel that I need to memorize more verses. Conversely, when I'm on the speakers' circuit, where I am constantly, I can get up and expound for a long period of time. I have found individuals, such as deacons and trustees, who are very involved in the church, who have no problem speaking at church affairs. But, they have considerable difficulty speaking on other subjects. Thus, we tend to perform to our self-image, which dictates our comfort level. I am learning to conceptualize, which comes easier to me, aspects of my Christian faith to strengthen my ability to speak at length and with confidence during religious activities. Part of the process of conceptualizing, or forming an image of me performing a task, involves me increasing my knowledge of the Bible. Increasing my knowledge in turn will improve my self-image as a Christian and speaker on matters of that faith.

Let me give you an example of having a poor self-image or low self-esteem, within a diversity context. Little known to many people, is the continuing poor self-image and identity crisis that exists among an increasing number of dark-skinned people around the world, because of their skin color. Although the practice of bleaching one's skin has been reported among African Americans, that practice is increasing among Blacks in some Caribbean countries, such as Jamaica and the Bahamas, and in South Africa. The belief is that a lighter complexion, influenced by American and European models of success and glamour, is a ticket to upward mobility, both socially and professionally, and to having sex appeal. A negative self-image is as devastating as a debilitating skin disorder. There is nothing wrong with enhancing one's appearance, but attempting to alter oneself so drastically indicates a form of self-hate. That self-hate transfers from individuals to others who share similar physical features. In America, many young African-American children are still heard "dissin" (disrespecting) one another because they are considered too dark. Sometimes the same thing happens when someone is considered too light. Thus, even the self-esteem of light-skinned individuals can be impacted, even as their skin color may be desired by many.

A similar situation exists within the context of gender. Some women in particular, although men can not be excluded from part of this scenario, have visited plastic surgeons and others to alter the shape and/or size of their nose, breasts, etc. For some reason, many individuals think that they will be happy by just altering their physical features. They even delude themselves for a while into thinking that they feel much better. But this delusion may not last, because behavioral patterns and personality traits often are too ingrained. Some people can't deal with the different ways people may treat them after such surgeries. They may wonder whether the person they are involved with, if it's a relationship they want, would treat them differently or want to be with them if they looked they way they used to look. Thus, there are other issues beyond appearance that can keep us from gaining a long-lasting positive mental attitude.

It's pretty much an accepted fact that whatever the mind conceives and believes can affect us in a positive or negative way. This brings to mind a number of stories I want to share with you to further emphasize the importance of having a positive self-image.

The first one, by an unknown author, has traveled the Internet. To paraphrase part of this story, it begins with an individual whose job was to visit elementary school classrooms, and encourage implementation of a training program for children. The goal was to empower students, using language arts, to feel good about themselves and take charge of their lives. When the trainer arrived in one classroom, she noted that the teacher was conducting an exercise in which she had her students filling a sheet of paper with thoughts and ideas. The visitor observed that the students were writing the same thoughts. They were all filling their pages with a list of 'I Can'ts.' Some of the statements on their lists were, "I can't kick the soccer ball past second base," "I can't do math," and "I can't spell." But it didn't stop there. The teacher also was listing her 'I Can'ts' with such statements as, "I can't get Johnny's parents to come to parent teacher meetings," "I can't get Billy to use words instead of fists," and "I can't get my daughter to put gas in the car."

This activity went on for a while longer, then the teacher had everyone stop, fold their papers in half and walk to the front of the room where they put the papers in a box. The teacher then picked up the box, led the students out of the room, stopping long enough at the custodian's office to pick up a shovel, and proceeded outside to the farthest corner of the school playground. There they began to dig. They dug a hole to bury the box of 'I Can'ts!' At this point, the teacher announced, "Boys and girls, please join hands and bow your heads." The teacher then delivered the eulogy: "Friends we are gathered here today to honor the memory of 'I Can't.' While he was here on earth, he touched the lives of everyone, some more than others. We have provided 'I Can't' with a final resting place and will add a headstone that contains his epitaph. He is survived by his brothers and sisters, 'I Can', 'I Will', and 'I'm Going to Right Away'. They are not as well known as their famous relative and are certainly not as strong and powerful yet. Perhaps someday, with your help, they will make an even bigger mark on the world. May 'I Can't' rest in peace and may everyone present pick up their lives and move forward in his absence. Amen." The teacher and students returned to their classroom and had a wake. They celebrated the passing of 'I Can't' with cookies, popcorn, and fruit juices. As part of the celebration, the teacher cut a large tombstone from butcher's paper. She wrote the words "I Can't" at the top and put RIP in the middle. The date was added at the bottom. The paper tombstone hung in the classroom for the remainder of the year. On those rare occasions when a student forgot and said, "I Can't," the teacher pointed to the RIP sign. The student then remembered that "I Can't" was dead and chose to rephrase the statement. Burying "I Can't" encouraged the students to explore relationships with 'I Can'ts' surviving siblings, who emphasized a more positive attitude.

My next story is personal. In a previous role as an undergraduate student I found myself flunking biology. Therefore, I did what most college students did in similar circumstances, I withdrew from the class just before the "class drop" deadline. I was always telling myself, "I can't do physical science." However, I knew I had to take the class again at some point, so I began preparations early. During the following Winter break, I purchased the biology book for the class I had enrolled in for the next quarter. This time around I read the book, although I wasn't quite sure I understood what I was reading. When the class started in the winter quarter, I studied at least an hour or two each day. I would ask the professor questions and do all of the assigned work. Can you believe I earned an 'A' in that class for the quarter? I succeeded because I took steps to enhance my image of my abilities, by embracing the "I can" feeling. I conceived it, believed it, so achieved it.

Another example I will use is a demonstration I use in seminars. I ask for volunteers and have either three or four come to the front of the room. I mark off spaces, each about 1 ½ feet wide, on the floor and tell them to pretend the spaces are balance beams. I have them walk on the balance beams. They first walk slowly, then I have them increase their speed, then even have them walking backwards. I then ask them how comfortable they are with the task. No one has ever said they were uncomfortable. In fact, they say it's easy. I then ask them to think of walking on that balance beam, that's now 5 feet off the floor. A few begin to feel uneasy at this point. I then ask them to think the beam is raised 10 feet, and then as high as the building we are in. The higher I raise the beam in their minds, the more uneasy they feel. This occurs in spite of the fact that the imaginary beam is 1 ½ feet wide. Very few now say they still feel comfortable. Again, the point is that what we conceive in our minds becomes our reality. The participants in the experiment usually indicate that they see themselves falling as the beam is raised. The volunteers feel uneasy because they know that if the exercise were real, they would actually fall.

What we are discussing here is visualization, which involves having a mental image of ourselves doing something before we actually execute the act. Another example may assist you in understanding this point. A while ago, I recall hearing a story involving a college football team. The team was divided into three squads. Up to this point, the entire team would practice daily for three hours, before an actual football game. Things changed. One group continued practicing three hours a day. The second group began practicing five hours a day. The third group also spent three hours on football strategy each day, but visualized playing the game for two hours and practiced for one hour. The question is, which group of players performed best during the real game? When I ask this question, most people respond that the group that spent five physical hours of practice performed best. However, you the reader of this book have probably guessed the correct answer. It was the group that spent two hours visualizing and one physical hour of practice each day. How could this be? Members of this group visually saw themselves, either on offense or defense, going over plays, catching the ball, intercepting the ball, sacking the quarterback, etc. They were actually playing the game in their minds. They subsequently acted out those scenes on the playing field. Thus, they outperformed the other two squads.

As I stated above, and you can probably deduce at this time, that self-image affects our attitudes and behaviors. Our attitudes about issues or situations are based on our beliefs about ourselves, which affects our self-image, which in turn affects our behaviors. These attitudes reinforce one another in either a positive or negative manner. Our behaviors are our actions or reactions. Motivation for our actions/reactions comes from within, and is based on how we feel and think about a matter before us. Our actions/reactions are prompted by external stimuli.

Because our attitudes are so important in the process of encouraging ourselves, I must spend a little more time on this subject. For years I, like many others, have been quoting noted civil and human rights advocate the Rev. Jesse Jackson when he says: "It's not your aptitude but your attitude, that determines your altitude. And all you need is intestinal fortitude." Additionally, one Harvard University study indicated that 85% of the reason for our success in life is due to our attitudes, and only 15% is attributed to facts, figures, and technical expertise. What is disturbing, according to noted positive mental attitude guru, Zig Ziglar, is that 90% of our education, from kindergarten through graduate school, is directed toward acquiring facts and figures, while only 10% addresses how we feel or our attitudes about various topics.

I believe another hindrance to developing a positive self-image is that the American educational system, in public and private schools, is still caught up in the "innate ability" theory. This theory purports that our inner, essential nature is determined at birth and there is little we can do to change it. Therefore, some of us will be "dumb" or "smart" based on where we were raised, our environment. A stereotype, that perhaps leads to a self-fulfilling prophecy, is that if we are poor and/or a person of color we will not fair too well in this educational system. I join organizations, such as the Efficacy Institute in Lexington, Massachusetts, that are emphatic about a genuine truth, that "smart is not something you are, smart is something you can get_and we can all get smart."

I wrote and copyrighted a rap for children in 1989 that ascribes to that truth. It's called *"Tukufu's Rap."* It goes like this:

Listen to the words I'm about to say,

Unlike Burger King, you cannot have it your way.

I came here today, to let you know,

Excel in school, it's the only way to go.

Don't let no one say you don't have the aptitude,

Just listen to Jesse, it's all about attitude.

So teachers I say, like Earth, Wind and Fire,

Meet them at their need or it's time to retire.

So home boy and home girl, stay in school and do your best.

Stay out the streets and all that mess.

Reefer, crack and alcohol, ain't right in school,

And if it's your habit, you'll always be a fool.

So finally I say if you wanna be chillin,

Excel in school or you'll only be illin.

Copyright _ 1989 by Darryl S. Tukufu

Thus, there is truth to the saying that "attitude is everything." We know that having a good attitude means thinking positively and having a great deal of enthusiasm. I know this to be true, because a number of contracts I have received to do either motivational speaking, organizational development, or diversity management was because I am rated highly for being positive and enthusiastic. However, don't think that knowledge and substance are unimportant. We still need these to even get into the qualified pool to be chosen.

Let me give you another example to show the power of attitude. Years ago, I heard one of the most dynamic motivational speakers in the world, Les Brown, recall a story about two guys working on a railroad. Another man approached them and said, "Hi Dave." Dave, one of the workers, looked at the fellow, grinned and said, "Hi Jim. How's the family?" Jim and Dave spoke for awhile, then Jim walked away. The crew member that Dave was working with said, "Isn't that the president of the railroad? How do you know him?" Dave told him that he and Jim started working for the railroad on the same day more than 20 years ago. The crew member didn't say it but thought, "Why is Dave still working out here in the sun, while Jim went on to become president of the railroad." Les Brown said the reason was because Dave went to work for the railroad for money, less than $2 an hour. Jim, on the other hand, went to work for the railroad. You see, to Jim it was more than a job. It was a career, a commitment. His work reflected his attitude and he progressed and advanced.

I look around today, while shopping at various stores, eating out at different restaurants, and occasionally stopping at drive-thru restaurants. I join a chorus of individuals who complain about the service. But we already know the crux of the problem. Many individuals are going to work for the hourly wage, not for the company. I have heard workers complain openly, in front of customers, about their jobs and their employer. Some even tell fellow employees that

42

they will refuse overtime, and can't wait for their work shift to end. Obviously, unless they change their attitude, they will not get any further in the organization than they are right now. That is to say, if they continue to be employed.

Finally, having self-esteem is significant in encouraging yourself because it involves accepting yourself unconditionally. You know you may have setbacks, bouts of self-doubt, but those are just a part of life. An African proverb says, "To stumble is not to fall, but to go forward faster."

Having self-esteem also means valuing yourself. We are all unique. This applies to twins, triplets, and even that person that someone says you look like. Just because you look like someone else does not mean that you also have his qualities, opinions and behavior patterns. Valuing yourself also means that you will not accept negative treatment from others, or react negatively toward someone else just because they are not like you.

However, the key to this issue of positive self-image is something that all faiths seem to have in common, and that is love. Love, in this sense, is having positive feelings about yourself, which can be transferred to others. If you don't have those feelings for you, who will? We need a healthy self-love that can extend to others around us. It allows us to reach out to others, and by doing so, we reinforce our sense of our own goodness and worth.

Now look back over your responses to the Feelings Inventory. Reflect on why you responded the way you did. Can you see why I included preferable responses? For every statement that you did not choose the preferable response, circle the corresponding number on the list below (or on a separate piece of paper if you borrowed this book)

43

and give two actions you will try to take to obtain the preferable response:

1._____
_____

2._____
_____

3._____
_____

4._____
_____

5._____
_____

6._____
_____

7._____
_____

8._____
_____

9._____
_____

10._____
_____

11._____
_____

12._____
_____

13._____
_____

44

14._____
_____

15._____
_____

16._____
_____

17._____
_____

18._____
_____

19._____
_____

20._____
_____

21._____
_____

22._____
_____

23._____
_____

24._____
_____

25._____
_____

3. SURROUND YOURSELF WITH QUALITY PEOPLE

"No man is an island," wrote John Donne, a poet who lived and wrote more than 200 years ago. Like I do on other occasions, I amend this to say "no man or woman," or "no person," but the amendment in no way alters what Donne was saying, that none of us operates entirely alone. That is to say, we don't meander through life in a vacuum. Individuals we associate with and groups to which we belong shape aspects of our personality and behavior. We cannot help it. No matter what our purpose, work, recreation, involvement in our faith, school, or family, we are in the company of individuals who have an impact on us whether we like it or not. Additionally, we have a need to be involved with others. If that doesn't happen, experts and research in the mental health field say mental breakdown may result.

Fellow sociologists and I emphasize the important role social groups play in society. We talk particularly about primary and secondary groups, networks, and reference groups. The primary group that we belong to is made up of close, intimate associates. This is the group where people have interacted with each other over a relatively long period of time. The secondary group includes individuals who have interacted informally during a shorter period. People in this group usually come into contact with each other because they have similar standings in society.

Networks are comprised of individuals who may be less familiar with each other on a personal level initially, but provide assistance on causes, careers and other areas where there is a shared interest. Although they have existed for a long period of time, networking and/or network organizations seem to be gathering more momentum. In my opinion, the foremost network specialist is George Fraser, an author and motivational speaker, whom I consider one of my mentors. He elaborates on issues we sociologists just touch on, like the importance of "webs of relationships" and establishing a sense of community among individuals. Most of us have heard the seemingly ancient saying: "It's not what you know, but who you know." We know that generally women and many people of color find it difficult to get ahead because of the "old-boy network," which keeps them out of places and positions. Fraser, in his books on the subject, and in network organizations he has formed, provides individuals with information and tools that will assist them to succeed in spite of such obstacles.

Reference groups are groups we "refer" to when evaluating our attitudes, behavior and status; in short, seeing how we measure up with others in a particular grouping. We check or evaluate ourselves against a range of data involving different aspects of our lives. The data can cover demographics, i.e., the region of the country or city we live in, or political, social, or reform organizations that we support. The focus of reference groups can be a matter of race, ethnicity, gender, class, age, religion, physical challenge, or sexual orientation. Or, it can involve education, work background, family status, military experience, etc.

In terms of size, primary groups are always small. Both secondary and reference groups can be large or small. Networks are considered social groups because they contain members from other groups, who provide access to those other groups. Additionally, networks can be large or small.

However, for our purposes, not only is the group association important, but also the individuals who compose

47

these groups, and with whom we want to cultivate relationships. To become successful we have to look at ways to adapt our behavior and attitudes to become part of the group environment we seek. It is in the above groups that we have the best chance to find the quality people we want in our lives, to help us develop the image we want of ourselves.

I use quality as a reference to character, or a characteristic that implies distinction or virtue. Quality people are not obstinate, self-indulging, or users. Neither are they, to quote groups like TLC and Sporty Thievz, "Scrubs" or "Pigeons," males and females respectively, who want to be taken care of by someone of the other gender. Additionally, quality people are not quality simply because they are members of your family, or social group. Quality people are not necessarily your best friends. People you come into contact with, even on a permanent basis, are not quality people if they tear you down in any way. If they say uncomplimentary things about your dreams or goals, or are a source of discouragement, they do not meet the standard of quality people.

I emphasized this point at a workshop I was conducting with teachers. I explained to them that if so-called friends belittle them and make disparaging remarks like, "Why are you teaching *those* kids," "Why are you teaching at *that* school" or "If I were you, I would ask for a transfer," then they are not quality people. I explain to students that peers who tease them for "talking proper," that is speaking proper English, or call them a nerd because they are smart in school, are not quality people.

I feel the best example of a quality person is one who exhibits characteristics found at 2 Peter 1:5-7. To paraphrase, this scripture says that to our faith we should add

48

goodness, knowledge, self-control, perseverance, godliness, brotherly (and I add sisterly) kindness, and last, but not least, love. I've highlighted each of these characteristics below.

Goodness is synonymous with righteousness. You can't go wrong interacting with individuals with this quality because they operate out of a sense of morality and the desire to do the right thing. They look for the good in people and are more likely to motivate you to be an even better person.

Knowledge, as in the prayer I developed, is also key. Knowledge is the intelligent input that a quality person would possess. Knowledgeable individuals are insightful. They can give you objective input about your status, and provide you with necessary information to keep you focused on becoming successful.

It is difficult for a person to talk to you about self-control if they lack this quality themselves. As individuals, we must be able to show some reserve or constraint, which can be difficult given the many challenges we face daily. Individuals who exercise self-control are important in our lives, because they provide us with the best example of how we should react in situations that try our patience.

Perseverance is also what I call stick-to-it-ness. Again, challenges may cause us to become depressed, overwhelmed, and extremely disenchanted. Having someone around us who seems to always bounce back from adversity, and always put her best foot forward, provides an excellent example in being diligent.

I remember reading an article some time ago that gives us more insight into this type of person. The article was about two men who were caught in an avalanche and had to virtually crawl back to where they thought they would find civilization. For awhile, they traveled together pressing each other to keep moving. Soon, one started moving more slowly. His friend tried to encourage him to keep up, but the other still lagged behind. He actually gave up in his heart, but told his friend to keep going, insisting he would be right behind. It began to snow quite heavily, so the lagging friend told his partner to be his trailblazer and make a path that he could follow. Well, his friend kept going and made it to a shelter. This man had no way of measuring the distance he had come, but kept looking out and calling for his friend, who never appeared. The next day the man who found shelter was rescued. A search party found his friend, frozen to death just 50 yards from the shelter. The one who persevered is like those individuals we need around us. They provide the example we need to continue in spite of difficulties.

Godliness refers back to having faith, because it requires action. It requires us to act in a divine way, conforming to the will of God. This doesn't mean that individuals with godly qualities will think or act like they are better than others. It means they reflect the qualities of the creator, by being kind, compassionate, supportive, etc.

Kindness reminds me of two attributes, being service-oriented and courteous. When people are courteous, we feel free to express ourselves to them without feeling we are being analyzed. Service-oriented persons make themselves available to assist us whenever help is needed. This reminds me of a saying attributed to the motivational speaker and author, Zig Ziglar, which goes: "You can get everything in life you want, if you help enough people get what they want".

50

The most important characteristic a quality person would possess is love. Love, for our purposes, is a genuine fondness that includes having understanding and mature acceptance of our imperfections. When we know that the people around us love us for who we are, it bolsters our confidence, which encourages us to take chances. And, love builds trust. We come to rely on quality people, who display love, to be with us through thick and thin, because they believe in us so much. They will not let us look down, but push us to hold our head up. Les Brown says, "Life may knock you down, but when it does, try to land on your back. Because if you can look up, you can get up."

Now, don't think that no one living today could possibly possess the characteristics I just described. They are around. But, also remember you and others reading this book can be the quality persons we need in our lives.

Quality people can be members of our family, members of various social groups we belong to, and can represent the diversity I mentioned earlier in this book. Let me briefly relay two stories involving family members, on this issue of quality people. One story shows how even a family member is not necessarily a quality person, and one shows how a family member can be just the person we need.

My wife recently told me about a lively discussion at her beauty salon, where one of the patrons, fresh from vacation, said people in the city she visited were distraught over the death of a 6-year-old girl. As the story went, the mother of this young girl had the girl's hair fixed up with braids and had some hair pieces glued together into quite a sharp hairdo, at the beginning of the school year. Everyone was quite proud of how she looked. However, her hair was not maintained during the rest of the year. There was no indication that her hair was even washed after this time. Her hair was free to grow on its own, with no nurturing. As the school year was coming to an end, a teacher in the school finally responded to complaints the girl had been making. You see, for some time the girl had complained about headaches. This teacher, a kindly older woman, parted the girl's hair the best way she could to look at her scalp. She saw that spiders had built a nest in the little girl's hair, and had eaten through her skull into her brain. When the teacher saw the girl's brain exposed in this manner, she had a massive heart attack and died. Two days later the little girl died. After details were broadcast in the media, the little girl's sister informed authorities that the little girl had been complaining for quite some time about headaches, but nothing was ever done. Their mother didn't respond because she spent most of her time abusing drugs. Thus, the children had to fend for themselves.

Unfortunately, there are many stories like this that we don't hear about. This is an example of a situation where an individual did not have a choice about the kinds of people in her life. Quality people did not surround this little girl. There had to be more people than the mother and her sister, who knew this girl's complaints should have been checked earlier. But no one moved, even at school, until one teacher began a preliminary investigation. The discovery contributed to her untimely death. Although family is an excellent place to begin engaging with quality individuals, this may not always be the place to find them.

But let's compare this story to one involving another family. The individuals in this story are good family friends. It is the story of Kimberly Ferguson and her mother, Betty Hines, who live in the Cleveland area. Kimberly has seen a number of tragedies in her life. Starting at age 15, fought and won a battle against cancer. At first, Kimberly's outcome looked bleak. For over a year she had to receive chemotherapy three days a week, with two days of in-hospital care. She lost more than 30 pounds, but she met each day with a positive outlook. Betty read everything she could that might help her child fight the disease. She wasn't going to give up on Kimberly.

Kimberly's cancer went into remission, but it returned during her freshman year in college. Her left lung collapsed. Doctors felt she could die before a lung was available, if something wasn't done, so they performed emergency surgery. However, they were in for two surprises. The first was that they not only had to remove Kimberly's lung, but they had to take part of her heart. The cancer had spread there as well. Secondly, during her first appointment after the surgery, doctors found that the cancer had completely disappeared. Both Kimberly and Betty said this happened because of their faith in God.

Kimberly went on to become a broadcasting star on Christian radio. She received rave reviews about her voice and her style of delivery. Wherever she went, people complimented her on "the fantastic job" she was doing. Although she loved broadcasting, Kimberly also had another desire, to be a wife and mother. She became both. However, as if she hadn't suffered enough, she had two miscarriages. Doctors added insult to injury by informing her that she would never be able to have children. But, as miracles had happened before in her life, Kimberly wound up giving birth to a son, Christopher.

But tragedy struck again. Christopher lived for only 6 weeks. In July 1998, Kimberly, her husband, Sheldon, and Christopher were involved in an auto accident. A motorist, traveling at a speed of more than 80 mph upon impact, struck them from behind. Kimberly and Christopher were thrown from the car. Christopher died and Sheldon suffered cuts and bruises. Kimberly lay in a coma for a week in a hospital, on life support, as a result of a severe head injury and fractures to her spine and neck.

As always, Betty was right on the spot. When doctors informed her that Kimberly's chances of survival were pretty slim, she did not believe it. She had heard this gloom and doom story before. She was going to keep on praying and working with her daughter, to help her recover.

Kimberly survived, but it has been difficult. Her memory from 15 years old and up was gone. She had difficulty talking, and could not walk. But alongside her, was her mother and others, like her sister, La-Tasha Stanley. Betty went from working full-time to part-time to help her Kimberly. She took Kimberly to a speech pathologist and physical therapist three times a week. Betty also helped Kimberly perform many basic household tasks, such as making the bed, cooking, and even getting dressed. It is obvious, that Betty, and others like her, are among the numerous examples of family members who are the type of quality people we need in our lives. With faith in God and assistance from her family, Kimberly is on track for a full recovery.

But the family unit is just one place to find quality people. In the last part of this section, I want to highlight other types of people who can be quality people in our lives. We can find them at work. They can attend the same educational institutions. They can be members of our various primary and secondary groups, networks, and reference groups. However, as I stated in the introduction to this book, we must possess a genuine interest in others who are both different and similar to ourselves. To find quality people from a different background, we must be open and ready to learn from and interact with people who may not be a part of our lives at this time.

I am aware of the prevalence of the 'isms' that exist in all societies, regarding race, sex, class, etc., to this day. These can present barriers to interacting with others, because individual acts of cruelty still ignite passionate feelings in us. I am talking about such cases as the one involving James Byrd, Jr., who was chained to a pickup truck in Texas and dragged to death by White men out to kill the first Black they came across. There were the two White males killed in Pennsylvania after they were kidnapped by two Black males in Ohio. Who can forget the case in the southeast where a White woman killed her two children and pretended they were kidnapped by a Black male carjacker? More recently, a gay man was killed by two "straight" males because one thought he was being propositioned. Even more recently, a Korean American and African American were killed, and other ethnic minorities wounded, because one White man wanted to die ridding the earth of "mud people." We are also aware of institutional acts of racism that result in discrimination in housing, banking, and the like. And Native Americans, even in 1999, are still fighting to regain land rights they unfairly lost decades ago.

However, we cannot allow ourselves to decide that we are going to only look for quality people within "our kind." I am saying this although, like most, I am endogamous. That is to say that I generally interact with persons within my racial group. My wife and, with a few exceptions, my extended family, are from the same racial and ethnic group. Most of us are like this. However, to decide to operate solely with those of "our kind" in all situations would be selling ourselves short in our quest to find quality people.

The following exercise will help you determine, and see first hand, the diversity of your environments. Originally, it began as a Bean Exercise used by many organizations, such as the National Conference for Community and Justice, to help people see with whom they tend to associate with in their lives. What you do is gather beans of various colors, black, brown, red, yellow, and white to represent the race or ethnicity of people. In my usual manner, I vary this exercise somewhat and use colored paper, similar to that of the beans, but I also add a gender dimension by using the stereotypical blue and pink colors to represent males and females, respectively. You choose the appropriate beans to represent your neighbors, doctor, minister, Imam, or Rabbi. The beans also identify your closest friends, significant other, the persons who own the grocery store where you shop, your teacher, and on and on. You will see how diverse your circle of acquaintances is by noting the dominance in color or variety of beans you amass. If you basically used one color, you likely are denying yourself the opportunity to meet quality people who are out there in various sizes, shapes, and colors.

To find these quality individuals, we have to first come to terms with our own beliefs and values. We need an open mind in dealing with others from a different faith, political sensibility, social or economic status, or race. There are quality people out there. We may have some difficulty locating them, but they are worth the effort. And, remember, we also may be the quality people others are looking for in their lives. But understand this, we attract to ourselves what we are. Who we have around us is oftentimes a mirror of ourselves. Do you like what you see in your mirror?

Finally, we don't have to have the same quality people around us all the time. Most of us tend to have certain friends at school, work, our religious institutions, our social life, etc. Of course, some of these friends may overlap into different groups, but I think most of us have "different folks for different strokes." I appeal to you to be open to different people, because you will find that you actually have more in common with them than you thought. Don't shut others out. Take a leap and sprout new wings.

4. DON'T TRIP

The use of vernacular, or slang, is common when we engage in everyday conversation. I call this section, "Don't Trip," because this phrase never seems to be out of style. I used it when I was younger and this current generation is following suit. The word "trip" here, is mostly used in one of four ways: "don't trip," "you're a trip," "you're trippin," and "you're tripped out". Although the latter usually implies that a person may be high on some drug, the others refer to a person becoming upset, most often because of worry, fear, or undue concern about risks.

Worry disturbs or destroys our peace of mind, because of recurring negative thoughts. Fear causes us to panic and anticipate that something dreadful will happen. The two are similar because they cause unnecessary stress. They differ, in that they represent different levels of responses we might have to a situation. For example, I know individuals who worry themselves sick when they have to make presentations before groups. They worry about the effect they will have on their audience. The fear would set in on the day of the presentation. Worry doesn't keep them from presenting, but fear causes them to pass the assignment to someone else, by feigning an illness, or simply refuse to make the presentation. Additionally, I know individuals who worry about flying or about driving over a bridge, but will do it nonetheless. However, if they fear flying or driving over a bridge, they will refrain from that activity, or go ahead in the rarest of situations.

As an occasional worrywart - and I'm working hard on this - I know firsthand that we allow many things get to us. We worry about our appearance. We worry that we'll be late to an event. We worry about our grades. We worry that we'll lose our job. We worry about our significant others if they are out too late. We worry about our children when they are out of our sight. Some of us worry more than we work. Worry can be more physically and emotionally exhausting than actual work. We worry, worry, and worry!

Worry keeps us up at night. Worry leads to high blood pressure. Worry causes ulcers. Worry can increase or decrease our appetites. Worry is a baaaaddddd mother (watch your mouth). I'm just talking about worry! And, unless we forget, worry can lead to paralyzing fear.

It's sad, but most of us are living our fears. Many times during the day, we think about them. They stop us from growing, developing, taking chances, and becoming successful. They hold us back so that we can never live up to our potential. We trip! Our fears have us in their grasp.

I've heard a number of motivational speakers refer to fear as "false evidence appearing real." There is evidence that it exists because of the way we react to it. This makes it real to some extent. If we firmly believe a bridge will collapse, that becomes our reality, whether or not there is evidence to support that belief. Our contention is false. But our imagination gives fear its power. Our imagination keeps us from moving up, and on. It tells us, like the story referred to earlier, "We can't."

Now, this doesn't mean that all fears are bad. To fear bodily harm is definitely common sense. But once you understand these type of fears, and have addressed them, you can continue to function. These fears will not immobilize you. But the fears that immobilize you are the ones that cause the problems. There is a difference between having a fear and the fear having you.

Not long ago, I spoke to a women's group about male-female relationships and the way many men enter into "connections" and "relationships." I talked about the difference between what I call the "social" man and the "physical" man. I have defined the "physical" man (See my book: *"A Guide Toward the Successful Development of African-American Males"*) as one concerned only with personal satisfaction. He has very narrow views of what a man or woman can or should not do; feels that females are only sex objects; and, prefers a number of short-term attachments, usually at one time. He finds it easier to make a baby than to take care of the baby, and insists on proving that most men are physically stronger than women, by striking them when challenged or embarrassed. The "social" man is the *real* man. He is defined as the one who believes that he and his woman are mates concerned with satisfying each other. He believes in egalitarian or shared relationships with the one having the most expertise, financial or otherwise, taking the lead in a particular situation. He believes that once a romantic commitment is made, the relationship must be monogamous. He understands that motherhood is a natural function, not a natural obligation, and understands and acknowledges that physical coercion is not acceptable, no matter what the circumstances.

The women in this group were quite enthused about the presentation and subsequent dialogue. I knew beforehand some of the fears and problems that many women faced in the group, so I went prepared to address those. I was pleasantly surprised when I later checked back with the group coordinators to find that one woman had a chance to address her fears immediately after my presentation. I was told that as I was leaving out the front door of the session, this woman's estranged husband was knocking at the back door. Typically, when she attended a meeting, she immediately would stop what she was doing and leave with him, when he came around, because she feared him. Their marriage was very unstable. They would be together a short period, separate, then start all over again. The women in the group were trying to provide moral support, but nothing seemed to improve the situation. But this time, bolstered by the discussion and interaction in the session I led, some of which dealt with confronting fear, she told her husband, "No, I will not go with you," when he showed up. This woman is working to get her life in order, by taking one step at a time.

Let me tell you. It is not easy overcoming our fears. But there are a number of things we can do to begin this process. First, understand that our fears are learned. This doesn't discount at least two fears we have at birth_the fear of falling and fear of loud noises. But by and large we learn our fears. Thus, we have to unlearn them.

Second, whatever fears you have, accept them and your responses to them for now. This means that if you accept them, you are acknowledging their existence. This gives you strength to resist. If you don't accept and acknowledge them you are doing yourself an injustice. Denying their existence allows them to persist.

Third, talk to yourself about those fears. Fourth, visualize yourself overcoming your fears and succeeding. I have to relate to you something I experienced on Labor Day weekend in 1998. I was fortunate to be selected to conduct a workshop at the Million Youth Movement in Atlanta. This was billed as a youth-run movement, which meant that those of us 30+ years old were few in number and weren't going to have roles in the various deliberations. My worry about the age difference became a fear, which surprised me given the numerous engagements I have had with youth over the years. I felt like an outsider and perhaps believed that whatever I presented would not be considered valuable, since I was considered "old." While preparing my presentation, I spent considerable time talking to myself and visualizing myself doing an excellent job. I began by telling me, "I can still relate to young folks," "I have something to offer," and "They will not diss(respect) me because of my age." And then I started visualizing, still talking to myself but saying, "I am going to stand up and present in such a way that they can't object to who I am and what I am saying." I know that my main fear was of being rejected by the young people in attendance. However, my fears proved to be baseless. The room in which I conducted the workshop was overflowing. But, I believe that what I did to prepare, such as talking to myself and visualizing success, helped me to overcome that fear and do an effective job. So I used my fear to build my courage.

Fifth, be willing to seek assistance in overcoming your fears. There are specialists out there who can help us. Don't "fear" seeking their assistance. It can be the difference between life and living.

Sixth, take the example from the burial of 'I Can't,' to heart. We must do the same with our fears. Write them down, bury them, give the eulogy, and celebrate.

Seventh, "keep on kickin." I remember hearing two versions about two frogs that fell into a bottle of cream (or milk..you choose which makes the most sense). At first they both kicked and kicked trying to get out, out of fear of drowning. One continued kicking, while the other gave up and died. The one that kept kicking eventually turned the cream into butter, then hopped out of the bottle. We have to "keep on kickin." We can't stop until we conquer our fears.

Finally, we can't trip, or become upset, because the risks we take may expose us to unpleasant consequences. An unknown writer wrote:

To laugh is to risk appearing the fool.

To weep is to risk appearing sentimental.

To reach out for another is to risk involvement.

To expose feeling is to risk exposing your true self.

To place your ideas, your dreams, before a crowd is

to risk their loss.

To love is to risk not being loved in return.

To live is to risk dying.

To hope is to risk despair.

To try is to risk failure.

But risks must be taken, because the greatest hazard

in life is to risk nothing.

They may avoid suffering and sorrow, but they

cannot learn, feel, change, grow, love, live.

Chained by their attitudes, they are a slave, they

have forfeited their freedom.

Only a person who risks is free.

So don't trip!!!

5. AVOID THE COMFORT ZONE□WORK

It has been said that there is no new knowledge under the sun, only the arrangement and application of it. I include this saying because I concluded the last section, *Don't Trip*, by discussing risks. Taking risks can also be a good way of avoiding the comfort zone. This book is one unit, but made up of different points, that overlap because of their relationship to the main topic. In this way, everything can be utilized to assist us in developing a positive mental attitude and preparing for the new millennium.

In this section I will offer ways to avoid the comfort zone, by stressing the need to work, on the physical and personal development levels, to become better than we are now in all aspects of our life. I will focus on difficulties we face in overcoming obstacles, and on our need for dedication, discipline and sacrifice, and the concomitant work it will take to succeed.

At the outset, we must acknowledge that most of us want things to be easy. We want no hardships in our lives. We want to be comfortable. If we can achieve something by doing very little work, we will choose that line of least resistance. Unfortunately, to some of us, our dreams are secondary to being free of challenges. If the going gets rough, we vacillate, we give excuses, we create ailments, and we blame someone else for our lack of achievement.

Face it! Life is hard! But I heard Iyanla Vanzant on the Oprah Winfrey show say, "If you don't have a test, you won't have a testimony." You see, life can surprise us at times. Anything can happen and probably will. We can be very functional for a long period of time and feel that things are finally going our way. And then something will happen that makes us feel like a rat on a cylinder. The rat is running and the cylinder is going around and around, but the rat isn't getting anywhere. But, it's got to keep running just to keep from losing ground.

But when we start avoiding situations, which may lead to promotions for instance, because they are too difficult, then we miss out on our potential for greatness. We can't be great at anything unless we overcome challenges. When obstacles get in our way, we have got to deal with them. There was a time in my life when I thought I would never become successful. I thought I would always be a "boy" or stuck in low wage positions. Most of my jobs from high school on up to young adulthood, had "boy" written all over them. I was a paperboy, a locker boy, a bus boy, a box boy, a key boy and I worked at a car wash. Now some would say that at least I had jobs and was out there doing something. Yes, but that something was not enough. Far too many people are comfortable staying in one spot, doing the same thing. This wouldn't be too bad if they liked what they did, or if they had a dream or plan to one day own their place of employment or start their own business. I wasn't interested in doing the same thing for life, even though I didn't know what I wanted to do yet. I attended Los Angeles City College during the "turbulent 60s" and flunked out because I spent more time in demonstrations than in class. And because I was in jail for assault and battery in an altercation with a University of Southern California student, I didn't take my final exams. I was in jail the weekend before exams, so couldn't study. It was during this time when I had what psychologists call an "S.E.E," a significant emotional event. I realized it was time to look at my life and start making changes. It took me some time to begin. But, eventually I did.

Many of us become impatient if change doesn't take place right away. But we've got to be patient and give ourselves time. Your time will come and even if "non-quality" people are around you at the moment, who would say they can't see you doing better, that's all right too for now. You must continue believing that your time is going to come.

Now, how you spend your time getting to where you want to be has a lot to do with that time arriving. I always ask parent groups and educators to identify which ethnic group, in general, they believe has the highest academic achievement in American schools. Most of them give the correct response, Asian Americans. This is not because Asian Americans are genetically superior to other races and, as my friends in the Asian-American community are quick to point out, all Asian-American students don't excel. Talk show host Tony Brown, reminds us that "in all races we have a few geniuses, many that are average, and a generous sprinkling of fools."

However, a documented record of achievement speaks well for the Asian heritage, which emphasizes strong family ties. That heritage emphasizes honoring ones parents, by being a source of pride to them, along with a strong work ethic. Early on, many of these students demonstrate dedication, discipline and a willingness to make sacrifices.

Many Asian-American students study longer hours than their peers from other ethnic groups, spend more time in the library, and more time preparing for classes. Far too many, but not all, other American youths spend more time on the telephone and partying. These youth seem to have the motto: "Party time is anytime and anytime is party time." It saddens me to talk to youth, whose only knowledge of a CD is as a compact disk, rather than a Certificate of Deposit. They have more of the former than of books, and many are dancing their lives away.

How we spend our time says a lot about who we are. If we spend more than three hours a day watching television after we get home from school or work, what are we saying about ourselves? If we can't get through a week without making at least two to three happy hours after work, what are we saying about how we value our time and health? If we spend two hours or more on the telephone, other than for business reasons, what are our priorities? If we spend time listening to gangsta rap and/or entertainment that's demeaning to women or other groups, what does this say about our conversation? If we spend two hours or more on the Internet, other than on self-development or self-awareness, what are we saying about our interests?

We can probably write off some of the above as bad habits. But there are others, like smoking and other drug abuse, law breaking, promiscuity, and overeating, to consider. We shouldn't take "smoking and other drug abuse" lightly. Many of us only show real concern about so-called hard drug use. According to humanitarian Dick Gregory, however, the two most addictive drugs are nicotine and caffeine. But listen to the millions of people who say they can't get started in the morning until they have a cup of coffee, and I don't mean decaff. These are destructive habits that we have to break.

If you have these habits and have made the choice to overcome them, the first thing you have to do is something I mentioned in an earlier segment_talk to yourself. You should acknowledge that your habits are in control of your life. And only you can convince yourself that it is time to take back that control. You have to convince yourself that you are "the master of your fate." You will be helped in this move by doing what? Yes, you guessed it, surrounding yourself with quality people.

Be aware that even though you have dedication, discipline and you are willing to delay your gratification, you will probably have to modify your plans because something unexpected may happen. If the unexpected happens, you must draw on your hidden reserves, your inner-strength, to get around the obstacle. During the process you may get angry, defiant, and resentful, or suffer some catastrophe, such as the death of a loved one. These things can knock you down, but you have to be able to rebound. Say to yourself, "The harder the fight, the sweeter the victory."

Finally, I want to address the whole question of work. You see, after avoiding the comfort zone and acquiring dedication, discipline and sacrifice, your effort will pay off when you actually begin to do your work. What is work? An anonymous writer says:

Work is the foundation of all business, the source of all prosperity and the parent of genius.

Work can do more to advance youth than his own parents, be they ever so wealthy.

It is represented in the humblest savings and has laid the foundation of every fortune.

It is the salt that gives life its savour but it must be loved before it can bestow its greatest blessing and achieve its greatest ends.

When loved, work makes life sweet, purposeful, and fruitful.

The above quotation emphasizes the importance of work, what it can accomplish, and that we must love what we do. It reminds us that simply having wealth is unfulfilling. I would go so far as to say that even the information I have set out in this book is not enough, if it is looked upon as mere philosophical utterances. None of this will work if you don't. Farmers can plow, plant, and water all of their acres, which is work. But, unless they complete the entire process, they will not see the fruits of their labor.

For many years now, newspapers throughout the country report on a yearly basis the number of individuals who are dissatisfied with their jobs. Research shows that most heart attacks occur around 9 a.m. on a Monday, at work. And it never fails to amuse me when people pay homage to T.G.I.F. (thank God it's Friday), thinking that everyone has the weekend off. These are people who can't wait to leave work, and no doubt dread returning.

I want to put it to you as plainly as I can. None of us will be able to grow, develop and have a consistent positive mental attitude if we work just for pay. You have to enjoy what you are doing. In order for this plan of personal growth to work, you must realize that there is no free lunch. Look at the millionaire lottery winners around the country. Many have problems they never realized they had until after they obtained their winnings. Few invested, to maintain their wealth. They looked at the winnings as a free lunch. But, that free lunch actually became quite expensive. Individual lives have been disrupted, marriages have broken up, and friends have become enemies because the lottery winners didn't bring in others to share that supposedly free lunch.

Our children need to realize there are no free lunches. When we continue to provide for them too far beyond high school and possibly the college years, we allow them to continue depending on us. Once an individual is in his mid-20s, I believe he needs to be on his own. The possible exceptions are those attending to a physically or mentally challenged family member. Plus, the young adult may be physically or mentally challenged, or she may be completing an education or training program in preparation of being self-sufficient. Entertainer Bill Cosby addresses this in a humorous way when he talks about exercising "tough love." The bottom line is we have to get tough with our adult children. And, you parents must understand that you have to let them go. They can't live your life for you and you can't live their lives for them. We have to instill within them a sense of independence, as much as we can and by whatever means necessary. However, don't blame yourself if your children don't make it the way you would have wanted or don't live the way you would have preferred. They have to be responsible for their own actions. You can only account for yours.

Now, I want you to stop and think about what you have read thus far. Think back to the sections on Reflection and Regeneration. What are your feelings about the subject of faith? What are your thoughts about encouraging yourself, surrounding yourself with quality people, don't trip, and now, work and avoiding the comfort zone? If you need to take a breather, do it now. You must get yourself ready to move on to the last two stages of this book, about setting your goals and objectives, and having a plan of action. This will take real work. If you aren't ready for it, go back and review sections that may help you in this process. If you feel you are ready_. Let's go!

6. SET YOUR GOALS AND OBJECTIVES

I know you're probably thinking, "This sure is a lot of work to do in such a small book." But that's all right.

Big things come in small packages. My interest has been to give you the preliminary information needed to get you focused and move toward charting your own course. I've said it before and I'll say it again, "You must do the necessary work to build your better future."

Additionally, you will detect something else. Up to this point, I have largely used "us" and "we" in my writing. In this and the following segment, I will move from the use of those pronouns to using "you" and "your" instead. I have put in the necessary time to develop my goals, objectives and a plan of action. I want to help you with yours.

<u>SCOB + 1</u>

Remember the process I developed for you earlier in the book? I'm talking about the SCOB + 1 analysis (strengths, challenges, opportunities and barriers_). Please refer back to both your responses, and those from individuals you selected to complete the questionnaire about you. You should now spread the sheets in front of you, in the manner that suits you. Some individuals type out all of the responses and spread them out on a large table. Others put the information on flip chart paper and tape them around their workroom.

Now, once you have reviewed all of the information at your convenience, which should actually be a number of times as you work through the process, then ask yourself the questions below and write your responses.

1. If I continue to do things the same way and make no substantial changes in my life, what kind of person will I be in the next three years?

When you are satisfied that you have exhausted all possible responses to this question, then continue to the next question:

2. If I begin to make positive changes in my life, in spite of the challenges I may encounter, what kind of person will I be in the next three years?

There is one more question you need to answer. This question is very important because your responses will be used to develop your goal statements. To make it easier for you, proceed to the section below on Goals and Objectives, then I will introduce that question.

You have probably heard it numerous times before, so prepare to hear it again...you must have goals, a target, a focus in your life! And, you must be clear and precise about what you want. An African proverb says, "If you don't know where you are going, any road will take you there." Without goals you are like a ship without a rudder, and an automobile without a steering wheel. You are out there aimlessly moving around, not knowing what you're doing or where you're going. Goals provide you with the blueprint you need to chart a better life. But most importantly, these goals must be your own and not someone else's.

Allow me to illustrate this. I use this exercise with groups I facilitate. It's patterned after an experiment French naturalist John Henry Fabre devised using processionary caterpillars. Fabre arranged a number of these caterpillars around the rim of a flowerpot in such a manner that they touched end to end. The caterpillars began their trek around the flowerpot. Even though their favorite food, pine needles, was placed in the center of the pot, the larvae continually marched around the rim for seven days and nights. They all finally died from hunger and starvation.

I vary this experiment with people, to make the point about the need to set your own goals. I ask for volunteers and, once they come to the front of the room, I select the leader. I whisper to this person what I want her to do, which usually is to move around the room in some geometrical formation, like in a square, circle, etc. I announce to the other participants that only the lead person is allowed to keep her eyes open. I then put the others behind the leader. Each one is instructed to keep his hands on the shoulders of the person in front. This part will vary if you have participants who are wheel chair bound. If they allow someone to push them, to get them started and to keep going, physical contact will be maintained among all participants.

After all the instructions have been given, the leader begins her trek. I let the volunteers go along for awhile, then have them come to a stop. All are told to open their eyes. I then ask them, "Who in this exercise had a goal or goals?" Sometimes they all say they did. I then have them announce their goals. You will generally find that the leader had the more focused goal, usually getting from one place to another. The others likely had such goals as maintaining their balance, praying they didn't run into anything, or avoiding a fall. But all usually agree that the leader had the real, focused, more precise goal because she knew just where they all were going. The others had to follow blindly behind. You can use this exercise and have the individuals perform just as the processionary caterpillars did, but this time no one would know where they were going, regardless of whether their eyes were opened or closed. They would just know, and be told, that they were going over the same spot over and over. But this is also instructional because too many of us treat life this way. We continue to do the same thing with the same result. Someone said that insanity is "doing the same thing in the same way but expecting a different outcome."

Thus, developing your own goals is extremely important. Goals give you purpose. They should be written in a general statement form, and say what you intend to do in your life. They should be challenging, but not unrealistic. The important thing here is that you must believe in the possibility of achieving them, and act accordingly.

There are a number of areas in which you can write out your goals. They can be religious/spiritual, physical, financial, mental, career, family, and travel, to name a few areas. The following are examples to get you started:

Religious/Spiritual:	To expand my religious/spiritual knowledge and understanding.
Physical:	To increase my strength and stamina.
Financial:	To increase my income and wealth.
Mental:	To minimize the negative and move toward maximizing a positive mental attitude.
Career:	To master my vocation.
Family:	To spend more time with my family.
Social:	To surround myself with quality people.
Travel:	To travel outside of the USA.

Now, let's consider the final question, in this segment. Your responses to this question, central to the process of personal development, should be written as expressed goal statements.

3. What specific actions must I take to reach my desired outcome?

Look at the goal statement examples provided earlier, as a guide. Write your responses so that they read like those statements. It may be difficult at first, but don't give up. Once you complete this step, you can then move on to setting your objectives.

Objectives are statements that are specific and measurable, toward meeting your goals. They are next in importance, because they are designed to get specific, quantifiable results, which will lead to the attainment of your goals.

Using the goal list given previously, I will provide you with a few examples of goal objectives:

GOALS	OBJECTIVES
1. To expand my religious/ spiritual knowledge and understanding.	1a. To read through the entire Bible each year. 1b. To read the *Daily Bread* each day during the year. 1c. To read (a specific number) supplemental books during the year.
2. To spend more time with my family.	2a. To prepare a monthly schedule of activities. 2b. To plan a vacation and get away weekends for the year. 2c. To attend at least one family reunion a year.
3. To master my vocation.	3a. To read one book and/or article each month on personal growth and development, organizational development, and/or diversity management. 3b. To attend one major conference each year about education or training in my fields. 3c. To practice presentation skills at least three hours weekly.

Do you see the difference between goals and objectives? Again, objectives indicate specific, though still somewhat broad, actions to be taken. They are not the strategies for getting results. However, we must move a step further to arrive at strategies to achieve our objectives. This will be covered in our topic, *Have a Plan of Action.*

7. HAVE A PLAN OF ACTION

The old saying, "plan your work and work your plan," is as valid today as it was when it was first uttered years ago. Up to this point, I think you have been provided with all of the ingredients you need for such a plan. Now, comes the time to put it all together and act.

Action plans are the strategies, or the more detailed "how," you will use to achieve your individual objectives. One of the best ways to develop these plans, and write them down, is to list the specific actions or steps to be taken, the dates for start-up and completion, and the resources you will need to meet your objectives and goals.

Using the examples of goals and objectives presented already, the following action plans have been added to complete the process you need to assist you in the attainment of *R to the Third Power*:

GOALS	OBJECTIVES
To master my vocation	a. To read one book and/or article each month on personal growth and development, organizational development, and/or diversity management.
	b. To attend one major conference each year with education or training in my fields.
	c. To practice presentation skills at least three hours weekly.

ACTION PLAN:

Steps to the taken	Date Start-up	Date Completion	Resources
Ojbective a.			
Research books in respective fields Research periodicals for articles	11/99	11/99	Bookstores Libraries

Decide which books to purchase, check out of library, &/or articles to duplicate	12/99	12/99	
Set reading schedule, begin reading	01/00	12/00	

Objective b

Research schedule of major conferences to be held in 2000	11/99	11/99	National & Regional Orgs
Analyze budget & determine which conferences to attend	12/99	12/99	
Pre-register for the conferences	01/00	06/00	

Objective c.

Purchase &/or rent tapes of different personalities; listen to them	11/99	12/99	Contact those I'm familiar with or were referred to
Prepare a regular schedule for practice	12/99	12/99	
Practice	01/00	12/00	

The above is just one example of what you can do. The time to act is now! Are you ready to "just do it?"

CONCLUSION

I realize that you have been inundated with stories, sayings, and work throughout this book. But there is a reason. There is yet another saying I heard many years ago. It is: "If I always do what I've always done, then I'll always get what I've always gotten." This book has been written to assist us, not only in preparing for a better life, but also to avoid what is called the "paradigm effect." The effect blinds us to new opportunities and a new direction, because we continue to repeat old patterns in our lives. We may suffer from this effect any time we make some of the following statements:

"This is how it has always been done."

"It's already been tried before."

"Our group is different."

"That's a waste of time."

"Our leaders want it done that way."

"Nobody would ever approve of that."

The problem too many of us have is that we have allowed our paradigm to become the "only" way to do something. We can't see it any other way.

It is my hope that you have been inspired and motivated to develop a larger vision. Few, if any of us, are doing all that we are capable of doing. All of us can do much more. Once we obtain this larger vision we will see ourselves differently. The challenges we faced from time to time, will soon seem like minor inconveniences. Additionally, others will look at us differently. People will approach us and ask, "What happened to you?" Tell them life is changing, and that as it changes, you also have to change. But we have to determine how much we can share with others at any given time. If they aren't going through the process of change themselves, or respect it, they will probably discourage us in some way. At first, we will find that we can only share our process of growth with those who are also trying to create this larger vision.

As we make certain changes, however, remember that we can't erase who we are, especially in a physical sense. So love and respect yourself for who you are, and how you look. We are different on a number of counts mentioned throughout this book, whether based on race, ethnicity, gender, class, religion, disability, sexual/affectional orientation, or age. However, we also are very similar in our desires for success and achievement.

Reflection is important. We have to see where we are to assist us in determining which direction we should take for the future. Don't go through this exercise just one time. Once you complete the assessments, go back in about six months and repeat the process. Some other wise person said, "Yard by yard it's hard, but inch by inch it's a cinch."

Regeneration is invigorating. It allows us to open up and allow faith to work for us. It assists us in establishing a closer connection with the Creator. Additionally, it helps us gain peace of mind through mental and physical well being.

Revitalization is stimulating. We realize we have to work on and encourage ourselves. Understanding that we can't perform in a vacuum, we begin to surround ourselves with quality people. We know we can't falter, or negative thinking will get in the way. Additionally, since there is no free lunch, we must avoid being too comfortable and continue to work, both personally and physically in ways that will benefit us. We then have to set our goals, objectives, and then plot our plan of action.

A formula to achieve your goals by developing a positive mental attitude has been presented to you. What are you going to do now? I encourage you to seek out others to assist you in your development. I will now close this chapter of our lives, as I did in my first book, by quoting an anonymous writer who wrote:

Life is an adventure, dare it.
Life is a beauty, praise it.
Life is a challenge, mean it.
Life is a duty, perform it.
Life is a game, play it.
Life is a gift, accept it.

Life is a goal, achieve it.
Life is a journey, complete it.
Life is a mystery, unfold it.
Life is an opportunity, take it.
Life is a promise, fulfill it.
Life is a puzzle, solve it.
Life is a song, sing it.
Life is a sorrow, overcome it.
Life is a struggle, fight it.
Life is a tragedy, face it.

RECOMMENDED READING AND/OR LISTENING

Brown, Les Enterprises, Audio Cassette Singles and Collections, Videos: *"Choosing Your Future," "Four Stages of Personal Growth," "Getting Unstuck," et al.* 1350 S. Ridge Road, Wichita, KS 67209.

De Angelis, Barbara, Audio Cassette Single: *"Confidence: Finding It and Living It,"" et al.* 12021 Wilshire Blvd., #607, Los Angeles, CA 90025.

Fraser, George C., *Success Runs in Our Race: The Complete Guide to Networking in the African American Community.* New York: Avon Books, 1996.

Fraser, George C., Audio Cassette Singles and Collections, Books: *"Race for Success," "George Fraser's Greatest Speeches," "For Your Success: Ten Guiding Principles of Power Networking," et al.* 2940 Noble Road, Ste., #103, Cleveland Heights, OH 44121.

Grossman, Ned, *How to Succeed in Life: Ideas and Principles They Don't Teach in School.* Shaker Heights, Ohio: Diamond Publishing Company, 1998.

Jeffreys, Michael, *Success Secrets of the Motivational Superstars.* Rocklin, CA: Prima Publishing, 1996.

Price, Frederick K.C., *How Faith Works.* Tulsa, Oklahoma: Harrison House, 1976.

Smiley, Tavis, *On Air: The Best of Tavis Smiley On the Tom Joyner Morning Show.* Los Angeles: Pines One Publications, 1998.

Thomas, Jr., R. Roosevelt, *Beyond Race and Gender: Unleashing the Power of Your Total Work Force by Managing Diversity.* New York: American Management Association, 1991.

Thomas, Jr., R. Roosevelt, *Redefining Diversity.* New York: American Management Association, 1996.

Tukufu, Darryl S., *A Guide Toward the Successful Development of African-American Males.* Richmond Heights, OH: The Tukufu Group, 1997.

Vanzant, Iyanla, *The Spirit of Man.* San Francisco, CA: HarperCollins, 1996.

81

Vanzant, Iyanla, *One Day My Soul Just Opened Up*. New York: Fireside, 1998.

Ziglar, Zig, *See You at the Top*. Gretna, LA: Pelican Publishing Company, 1977.

Ziglar, Zig, *Over the Top*. Nashville: Thomas Nelson Publishers, 1997.

Darryl S. Tukufu, Ph.D.   **Hatcher & Fell Photography**

ABOUT THE AUTHOR

Darryl S. Tukufu, a husband, father, sociologist, and human resource consultant who with keen business acumen and "eye on the future" leadership has qualified him to serve effectively in numerous positions all over the United States. He was involved in the civil and human rights struggle, and has served in positions as a non-profit President and CEO, a local government official, and college or university professor and administrator. Currently, he is President of The Tukufu Group, a human resource consultant business specializing in personal growth and development, organizational development, and diversity management.

Dr. Tukufu's career as a sought-after speaker, facilitator, and workshop/seminar presenter has evolved significantly-largely due to his humanistic approach to problem solving and his ability and determination to help people achieve better human relations with one another.

He is a published author credited with *"Tukufu's Rap,"* a motivational rap for students; *"Jesse Jackson and the Rainbow Coalition: Working Class Movement or Reform Politics?"* an article in the May, 1990 edition of *Humanity and Society*; his first self-published book *A Guide Toward the Successful Development of African-American Males*; and this self-published book.

R to the Third Power is an important book written by a man that walks his talk. Darryl Tukufu has climbed the highest mountains and negotiated the lowest valleys to achieve success in his life. His generosity and commitment to openly share his knowledge and experiences in this insightful new book, will impact for generations to come, those who are smart enough to read it. It is written in a style that is concise, heartfelt and easy to understand. Dr. Tukufu's ideas are not only important, but usable in ways rarely found in books that inspire us. I highly recommend that you act on his guidance for your continued success. Bravo Darryl Tukufu for providing us a literary gem.

George C. Fraser
Author, *Success Runs In Our Race* and *Race for Success*

There are self-help and motivational books on the shelves; then there's *R to the Third Power*. This insightful book is more than positive thinking. Action is required. This may be the new paradigm of the next millennium.

David Namkoong, Founding President, Asian/Pacific American Federation; Vice President Communication, National Organization of Chinese Americans
Frances Namkoong, Former Vice President, Public Affairs, National Organization of Chinese Americans

Dr. Darryl Tukufu has articulately challenged his readers to leave their COMFORT ZONE and face life's hurdles. GREAT BOOK! A must if you're serious about a success-

85

ful, happy life. We are honored to have Dr. Tukufu as one of our SpeakersPlus speakers.

Tonnie Alliance, President of Operations
Arlene Schreiber, President of Sales Speakers Plus

In *R to the Third Power*, Dr. Darryl Tukufu addresses one of the basic human wants; the desire to become better, to do more, to realize our true potential. The reader is guided through the process of discovering where they are, shown the importance of Faith in any major transformation, and provided practical tools to take action and change. Dr. Tukufu makes a positive contribution to the self-improvement genre.

Leo Serrano, Former Executive Director
Spanish American Committee

As a senior in high school, your future could appear pretty bleak if you don't have yourself together. Dr. Tukufu's book provided me with tools for life that helped me set goals and objectives, and have faith in myself. If it can encourage a senioritis plagued senior to step up and tackle the world, it can encourage you.

Lauren Gaffney, senior
Cleveland Heights High School